UNIVERSITY OF OXFORD

· PIERO DI COSIMO'S ·
· THE FOREST FIRE ·

ASHMOLEAN MUSEUM OXFORD 1984

ISBN 090 7849 07 5

Designed by Peter Miller
Set in Garamond and printed by Cheney and Sons Ltd.,
Banbury, Oxon, England. 1984.

PREFACE

The Forest Fire by Piero di Cosimo is one of the most famous pictures in the Ashmolean Museum. This booklet is intended to provide more information about the artist, the painting, and its subject-matter. As such, it matches the publication on *The Hunt in the Forest* by Paolo Uccello (1981). Like that booklet, this too was initiated by a small didactic exhibition arranged around the picture by the present writer. Unfortunately it has taken longer to effect the transformation from exhibition into print and it is only through the kind and generous assistance of Ann Jones, a student who read for the Diploma in The History of Art in Oxford in 1982-3, and through the timely intervention of Sarah Shalgosky, a graduate in the History of Art from the University of East Anglia, that this booklet has been brought to a finish. I am indebted to Ann Jones and Sarah Shalgosky for their hard work and diligent efforts.

C.L. 1984

THE ARTIST AND HIS STYLE

PIERO di Cosimo (PLATE 1) was born (c.1461-2) in Florence, the son of Lorenzo di Piero Antonio, a metalworker. As his name implies, Piero di Cosimo was apprenticed to the Florentine painter Cosimo Rosselli whom he assisted in the execution of the fresco *The Sermon on the Mount and the Healing of the Leper* on the walls of the Sistine Chapel (1481/2). His style of painting forms a link between the Early and the High Renaissance and in this respect Piero di Cosimo's contribution to Florentine painting runs parallel to that of his contemporaries Botticelli, Filippino Lippi, Signorelli, and Leonardo da Vinci, whose works are often echoed in Piero de Cosimo's own. He died in 1521.

The small altarpiece of *Virgin and Child with Saints Peter, John the Baptist, Nicholas of Bari and Dominic* (PLATE 2), executed for the Pugliese chapel in the church of St. Spirito, Florence, is representative of Piero di Cosimo's early style. There is still a certain dependence on quattrocento principles. The saints are symmetrically placed on either side of the Virgin and Child with the heads of Saints Peter and John the Baptist carefully aligned with the Virgin's head. Their gestures emphasise the strong vertical axis, while the landscape background has not yet become an integral part of the composition. The light, entering the picture from the left, is sharp and intense. It helps to delineate the features of the figures and to enliven the draperies. *The Visitation* (PLATE 3), painted between 1485-95, reveals Piero di Cosimo's debt to contemporary Flemish painting, particularly to Hugo van der Goes, whose *Portinari Altarpiece* (PLATE 4) was set up in the hospital church of St. Maria Nuova, Florence, in 1483. Piero di Cosimo's combination of meticulous observation and forceful characterisation is here particularly evident in the figures of Saints Nicholas of Bari and Anthony Abbot in the foreground. Towards the end of the century, however, there is a change in Piero di Cosimo's style. The altarpiece, *Virgin and Child with Saints Catherine of Alexandria, Rosa of Viterbo, Peter and John the Evangelist* (PLATE 5), painted once more at the behest of the Pugliese family, but this time for the Ospedale degli Innocenti, Florence, has a greater sense of movement and rhythm than the St. Spirito altarpiece. It is a much larger work and the viewing point is higher.

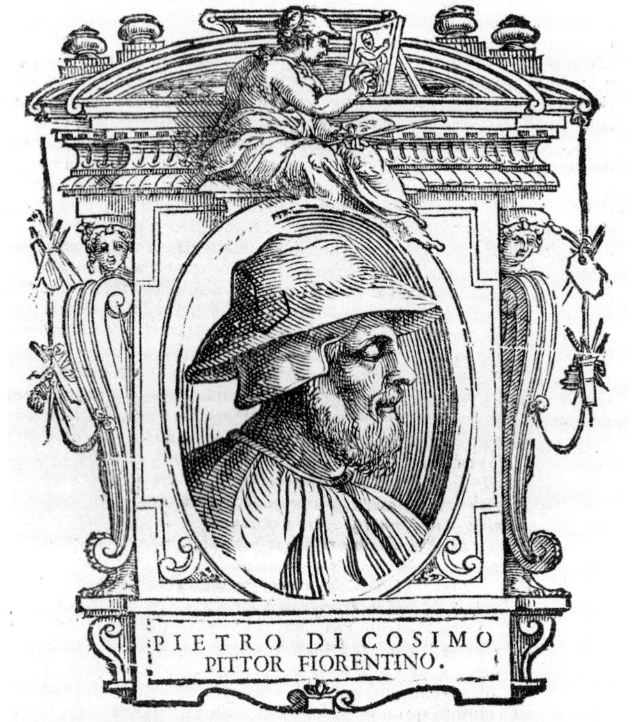

PLATE 1

PLATE 2

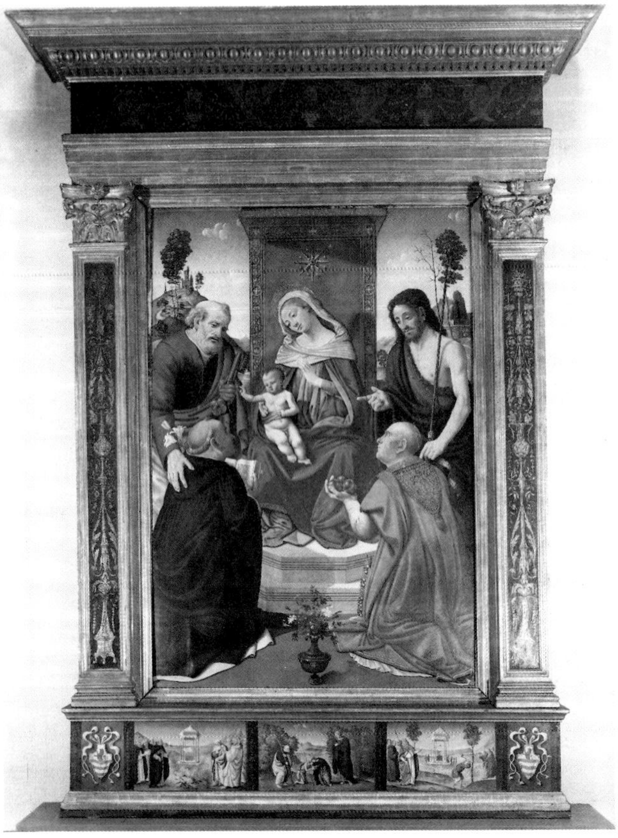

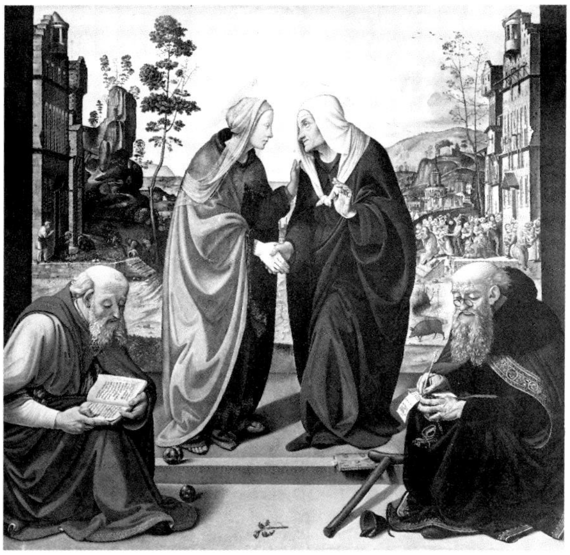

PLATE 3

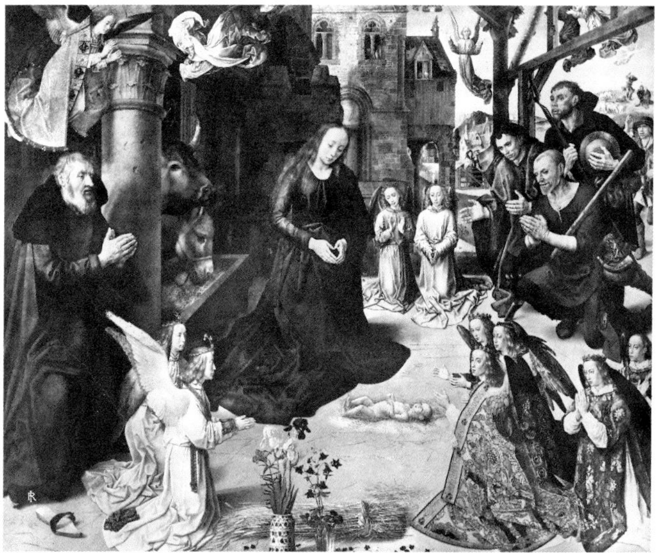

PLATE 4

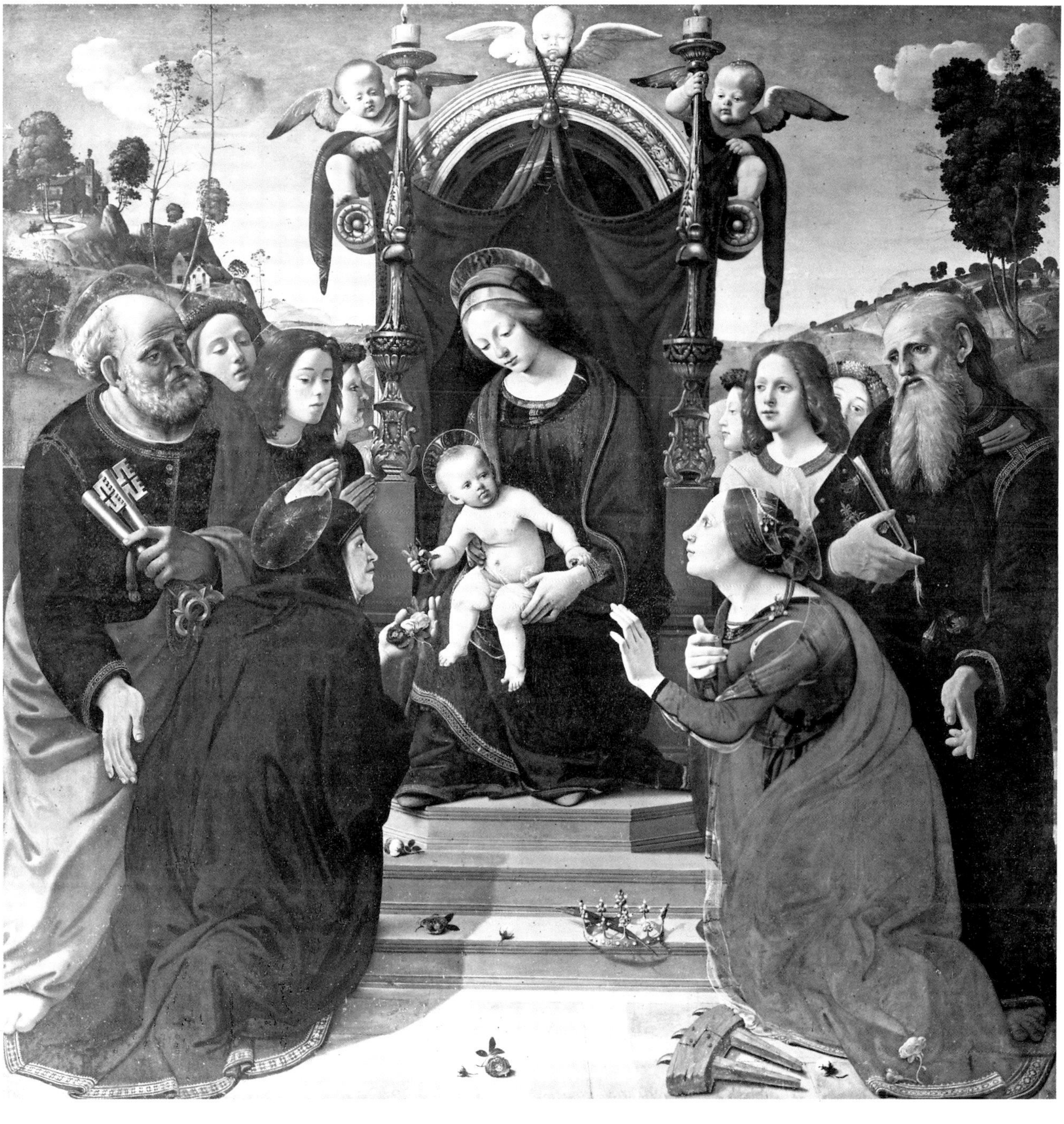

LATE 5

Furthermore, the spectator seems to form part of the circle of figures surrounding the Virgin. The treatment of the landscape also shows how the artist has learnt to make the background play a more positive role in the composition with the shallow diagonals of the hills on either side gently leading the eye into the centre. Such a composition demonstrates how the artist was beginning to paint in a High Renaissance style. The final phase of Piero de Cosimo's adoption of High Renaissance principles occurs in the *Virgin and Child with Angels* (PLATE 6), in the Cini Collection, Venice, painted towards the end of the first decade of the sixteenth century. Here the pose of the music-making angel on the left, derived from Leonardo da Vinci's famous composition of *Leda*, is carefully related to the circular grouping of the figures, which also owes much to Raphael's series of Madonnas painted in Florence between 1504-8. The composition is unified, with each part skilfully integrated, so that to remove one part would be to ruin the effect of the whole. Balance and harmony are achieved by the careful moulding of the interrelated figures, and in doing this Piero di Cosimo has moved well beyond the additive compositions of his early work painted in a quattrocento style.

Vasari gives a most enjoyable and lively account of the artist in his *Life of Piero di Cosimo* which remains the principal source for our knowledge of the painter and of his works. Vasari's character study is so vivid that he depicts a man whose eccentricities are more closely akin to the romantic conception of artistic genius, best exemplified in nineteenth century literature, than to the Italian Renaissance.

'The peculiarities of Piero's character became more strikingly manifest after the death of Cosimo, seeing that he thenceforward kept himself constantly shut up, he would not permit any one to see him work, but lived the life of a wild beast rather than that of a man. He would never suffer his rooms to be swept, and would eat just at such moments as he felt hungry, he would not have the soil of his garden cultivated, or the fruit-trees pruned, but suffered the vines to grow wild, and permitted their shoots to extend over the paths, neither would he have the fig or other trees properly trained and attended to, preferring to see all things wild and savage about him, as he was himself, and he used to say that every thing of that kind was better left to Nature, to be tended by herself alone without further consideration. He would sometimes set himself to seek animals, plants, or other productions out of the common order, such as Nature will sometimes bring forth either by chance or from caprice. In these things he took indescribable pleasure, insomuch that they transported him out of himself, and he would describe them so frequently, that even to persons who could take pleasure in such narratives, the relation at length became tedious and troublesome. He would sometimes stand beside a wall, against which various impurities were cast, and from these he would image forth the most singular scenes, combats of horses, strangely ordered cities, and the most extraordinary landscapes that were ever seen; he did the same thing with the clouds of the sky also . . .

'His inquiries into the more recondite properties of Nature, in her external forms, were conducted with a zeal that rendered him regardless of the amount of time or labour bestowed on whatever might be the matter in hand. While seeking to penetrate the secrets of his art, no effort was too severe; he would endure any hardship for the mere love which he bore to the pursuit, and in the hope of obtaining an advantage for the vocation of his choice. Piero di Cosimo was indeed so earnestly devoted to the interests of art as to become totally regardless of himself and his personal convenience, insomuch that he would allow himself no better food than hard eggs, and, to save firing, he cooked these only when he had prepared a fire to boil his glues, varnishes &c.; nor would he cook them even thus by six or eight at a time, but boiled them by fifties; he would then set them apart in a basket, and ate them at any moment when he felt the necessity for food . . .

'Piero di Cosimo was extremely amusing and varied in conversation, and would sometimes say things so facetious and original that his hearers would be ready to die with laughing: but when he had attained to old age, and was near his eightieth year, he became so strangely capricious that no one could endure to be with him. He would not suffer even his scholars to be about him, so that his unsocial rudeness of manner caused him to be destitute of all aid in the helplessness of his age. He would sometimes be seized with a desire to get to his work, when, his palsied state preventing him, he would fall into fits of rage, and labour to force his trembling hands to exertions of which they were no longer capable: while thus raving or muttering, the mahl stick would drop from his grasp, or even the pencils themselves would fall from his fingers, so that it was pitiable to behold.'[1]

It is hardly surprising that an artist with these characteristics should have exhibited such a wide variety of interests in his painted works and his oeuvre incorporates mythological pictures of great diversity (PLATES 7 and 8), in addition to the more traditional religious subjects. *The Forest Fire* is further testimony to Piero di Cosimo's highly individual approach to his art.

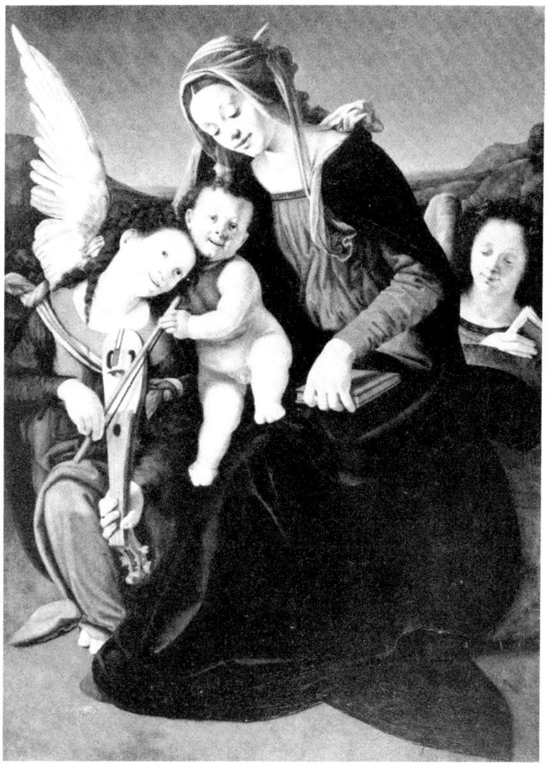

PLATE 6

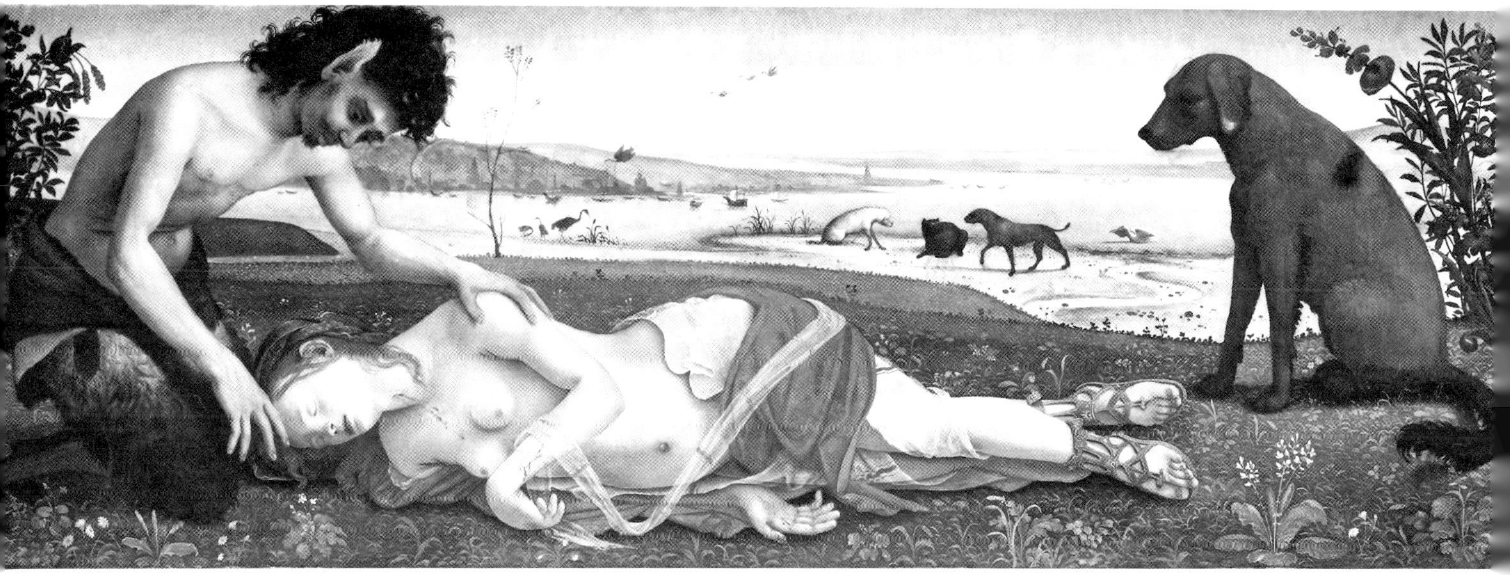

PLATE 7

PLATE 8

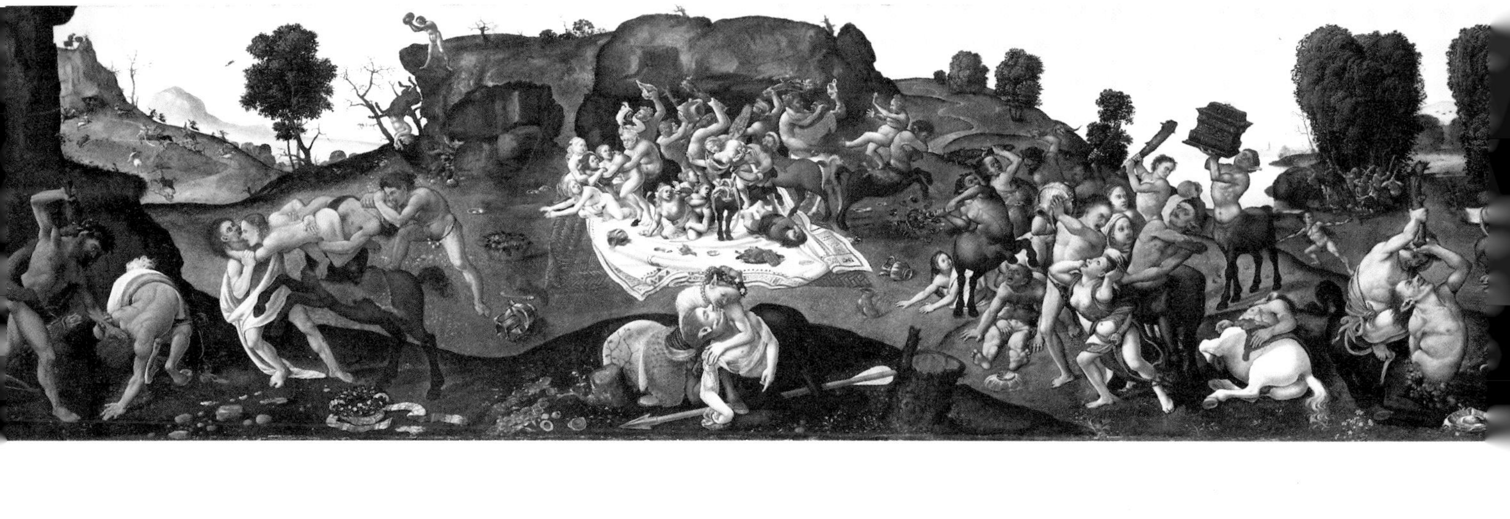

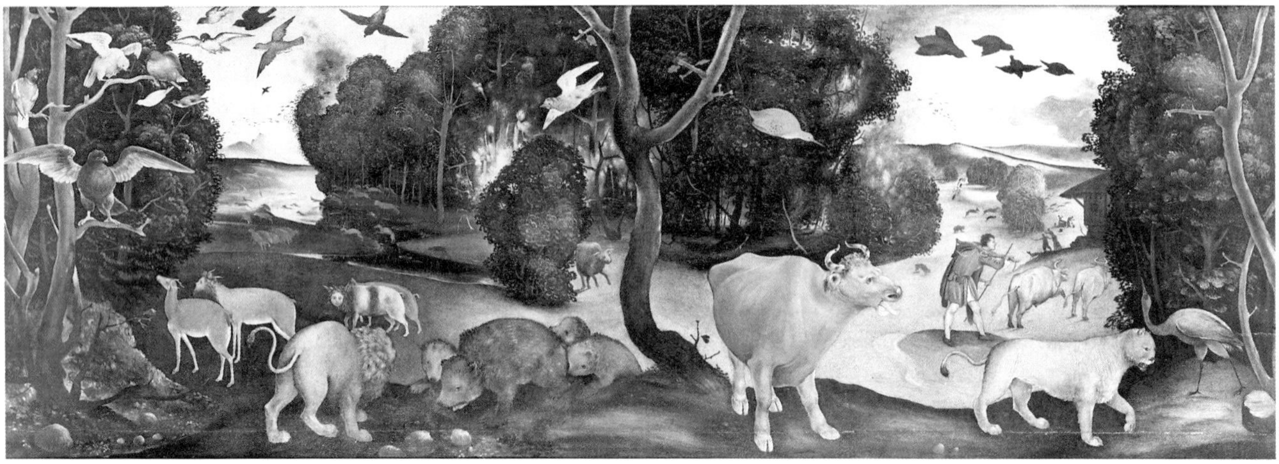

THE PICTURE AND ITS SUBJECT

(reproduced in colour on the Centre Pages)

The Forest Fire dates from about 1505. Stylistically, one of the chief characteristics of the picture is the even, creamy texture of the paint that betokens Piero di Cosimo's desire for a high finish, said by Vasari to have been inspired by Leonardo da Vinci. It measures 71.2 × 202 cm. and is in a comparatively good condition for a painting of such a date. Paintings of this size are very often described as *cassoni* panels which decorated the front of wooden chests specially made for the occasion of a marriage. The dimensions of *The Forest Fire*, like those of Paolo Uccello's *Hunt in the Forest*, are too large for the painting ever to have been inserted into the front of a *cassone* chest. It is more likely that *The Forest Fire* formed part of an elaborate decorative scheme in a private apartment where panels were inserted into furniture, the friezes and the *spalliere*. Schemes of this type are occasionally described by Vasari, an example being the bedroom of Pierfrancesco Borgherini mentioned in his *Lives of Andrea del Sarto, Granacci, Pontormo* amongst others. It has been argued at some length by the distinguished art historian Erwin Panofsky that *The Forest Fire* was painted for a comparable scheme in the Pugliese household, briefly mentioned by Vasari.

Panofsky connected *The Forest Fire* with a number of other paintings which he believed formed a series illustrating the history of primordial man. The related paintings are *The Hunt* (PLATE 9) and *The*

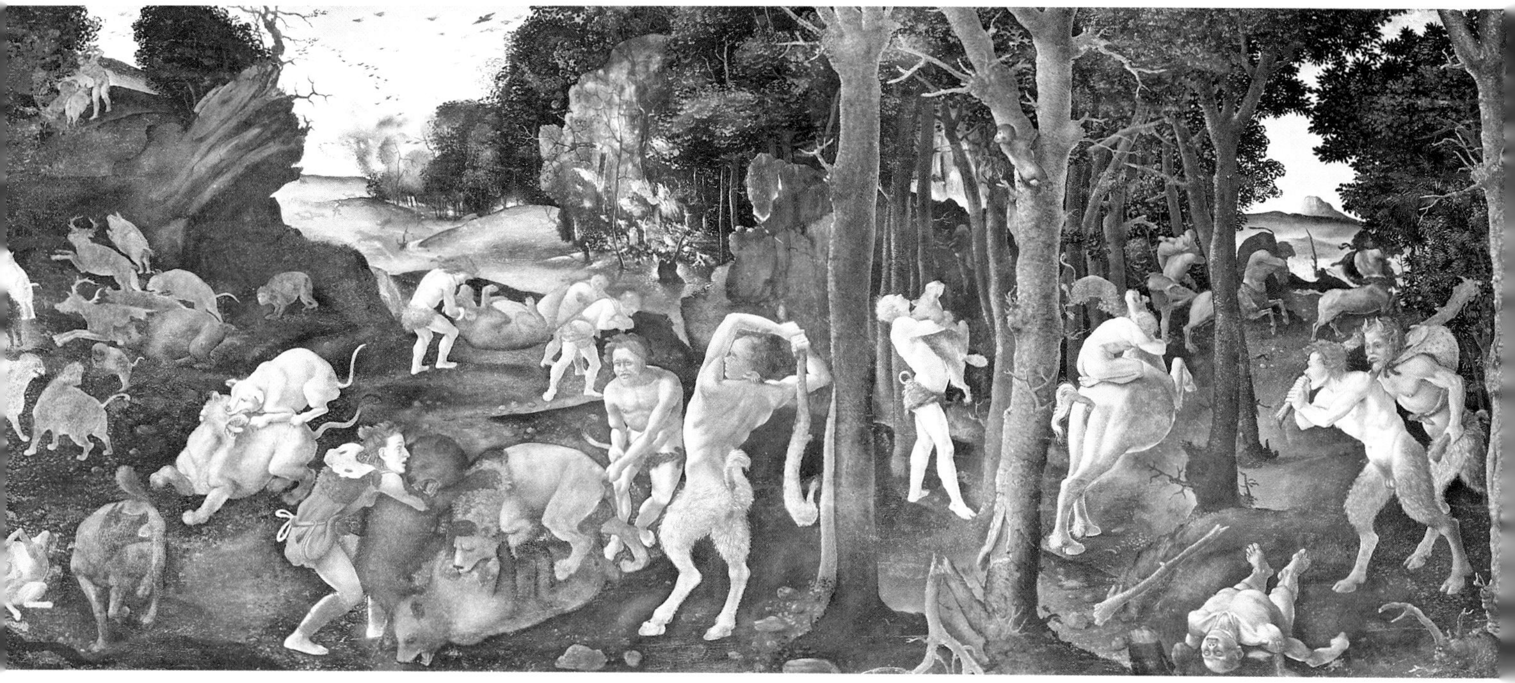

PLATE 9

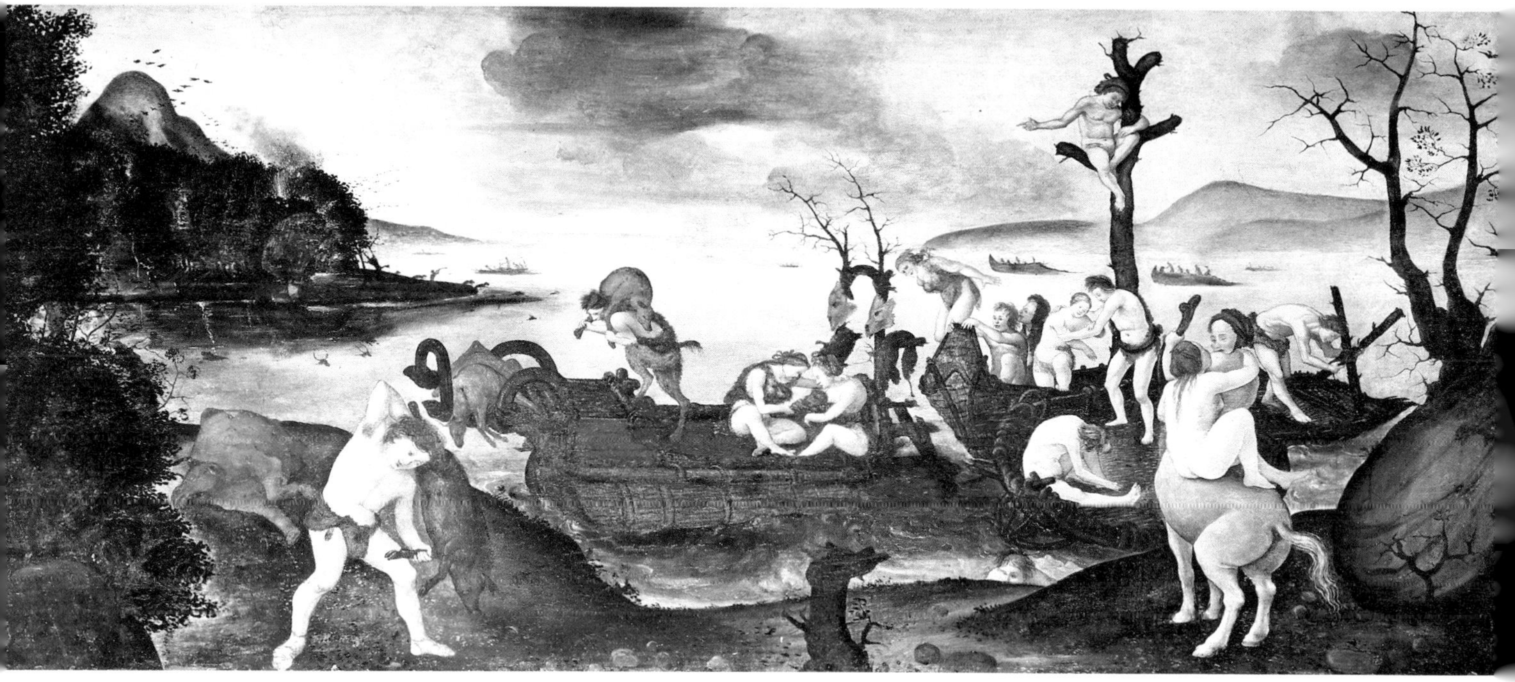

PLATE 10

Return from the Hunt (PLATE 10), both in the Metropolitan Museum, New York, *The Finding of Vulcan on Lemnos* (PLATE 11) in the Wadsworth Athenaeum, Hartford, Connecticut, and *Vulcan and Aeolus* (PLATE 12) in the National Gallery, Ottawa. The two pictures in New York depict man's life in its most primitive stages, before the technical and social advantages of the teachings of Vulcan, the ancient god of fire, became apparent. Man is therefore seen hunting without the aid of metal weapons and has not yet built any developed form of habitation. It is a brutal, primitive world in which man lives in a manner resembling that of the animals he kills. Fire rages in the background, but it is not used because its advantages remain unknown. In *The Forest Fire* there are signs that man has reached a slightly more advanced stage, as the figure on the right carries a wooden yoke and seems to be returning to a primitive hut, but more importantly, the picture's main subject is the discovery of fire. The other two paintings,

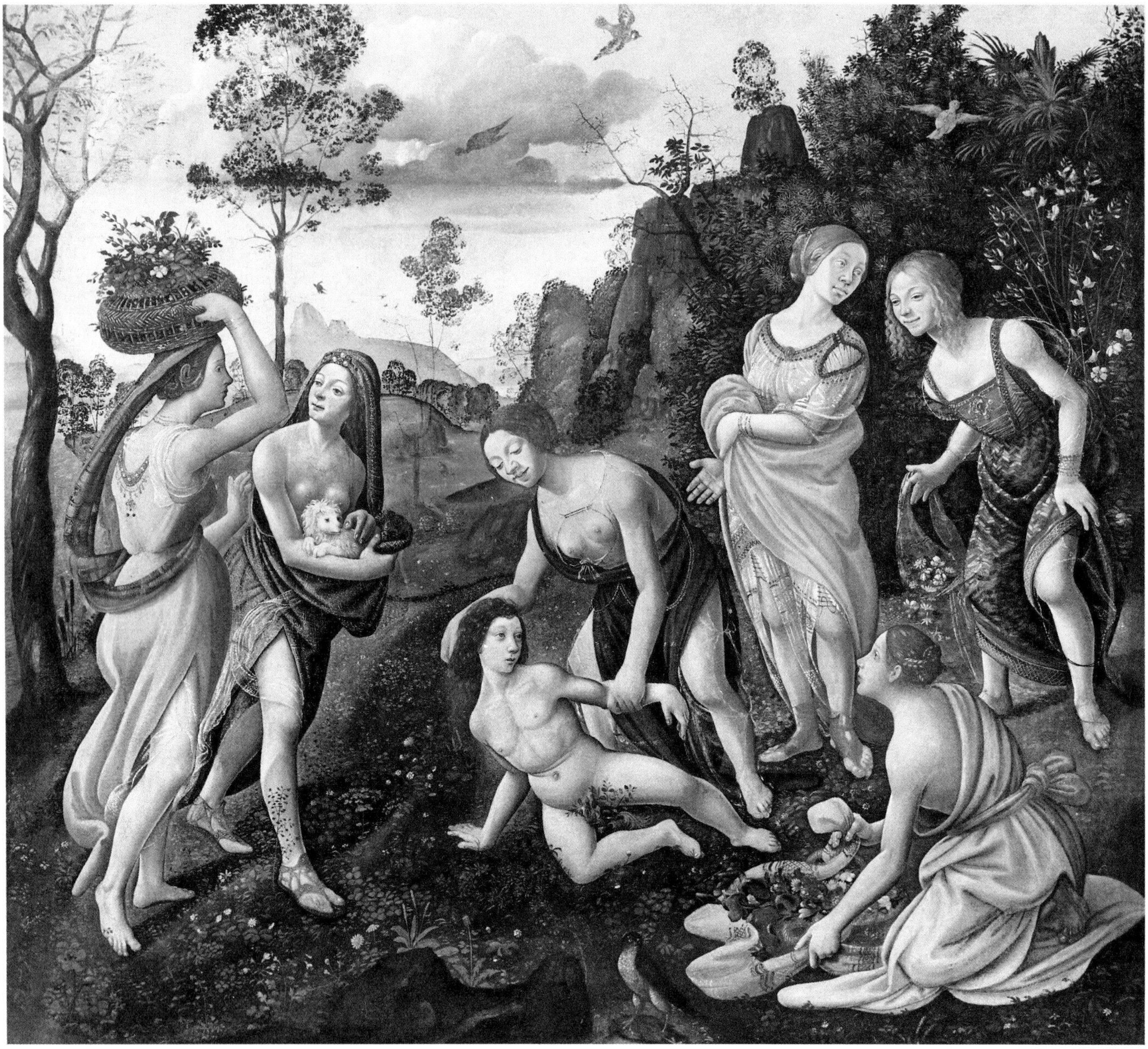

PLATE 11

The Fall of Vulcan and *Vulcan on Lemnos*, show a more developed way of life where, under the guidance of Vulcan, man has learned to use fire for the betterment of his condition and way of life. Thus, as Panofsky commented, *The Forest Fire* is concerned with the middle stage in the evolution of man, portraying 'a transition from the unmitigated bestiality to a comparatively human life'. Piero di Cosimo's fascination for the subject of primitive society is displayed in other paintings such as *The Myth of Prometheus* (Strasbourg and Munich), *The Discovery of Honey* (Worcester, Massachusetts) and *The Building of a Palace* (Ringling Museum, Sarasota), but these do not form part of the series under discussion.

The mythology of the discovery of fire is recounted in the oral and written traditions of many early civilisations. The Elder Pliny, Lucretius, and Diodorus Siculus are amongst the ancient authors who record these myths, but Piero di Cosimo was probably more conversant with the account given by Vitruvius in *De Architectura* (Book II i.ff.), because the relevant passage was quoted by Giovanni Boccaccio in *Della Genealogia Deorum* (Book XII. lxx), which was one of the most popular written sources used by Renaissance artists. Vitruvius records the discovery of fire as follows:

'In the olden days men were born like wild beasts in woods and caves and groves, and kept alive by eating raw food. Some-

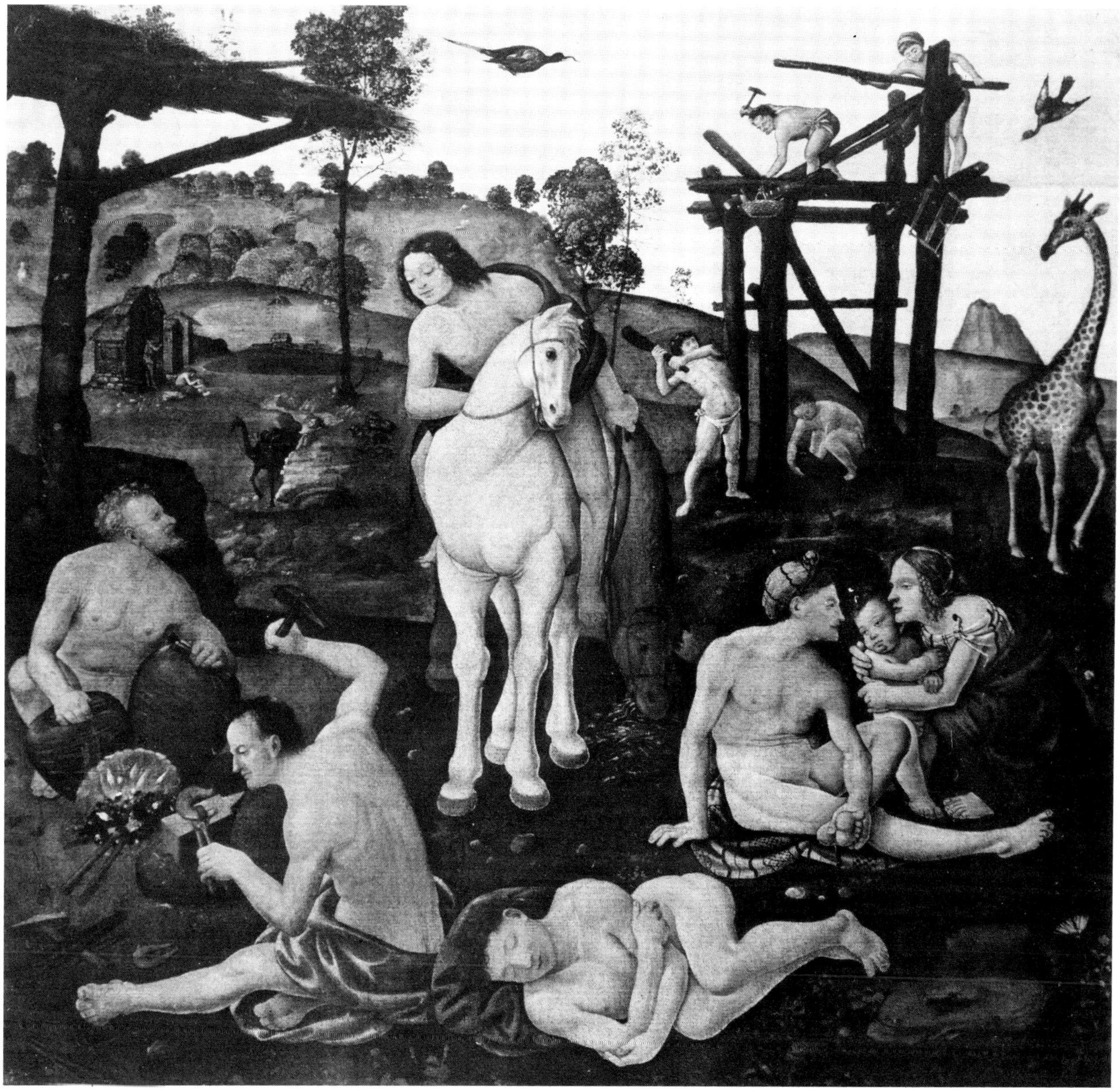

PLATE 12

PLATE 13

where, meanwhile, the close-grown trees tossed by storms and winds rubbing their branches together caught fire. Terrified by the flames those near the spot fled. When the fire subsided, they drew near, and since they noticed how pleasant to their bodies was the warmth of the fire, they laid on wood; and thus keeping it alive, they brought up some of their fellows and, indicating the fire with gestures, they showed them the use they might make of it'.

Most illustrated editions of Vitruvius contained woodcuts depicting this account of the discovery of fire (PLATE 13). In *The Forest Fire* Piero di Cosimo has shown creatures fleeing in fear from the flames, and it is possible that he was familiar with this passage and contemporary illustrations of it.

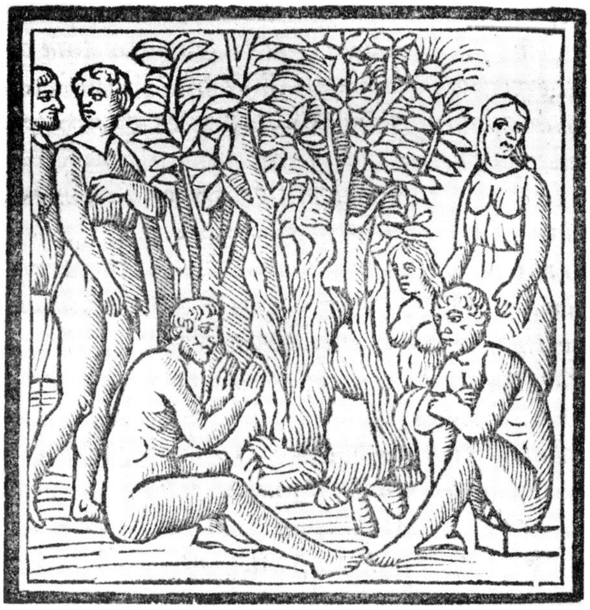

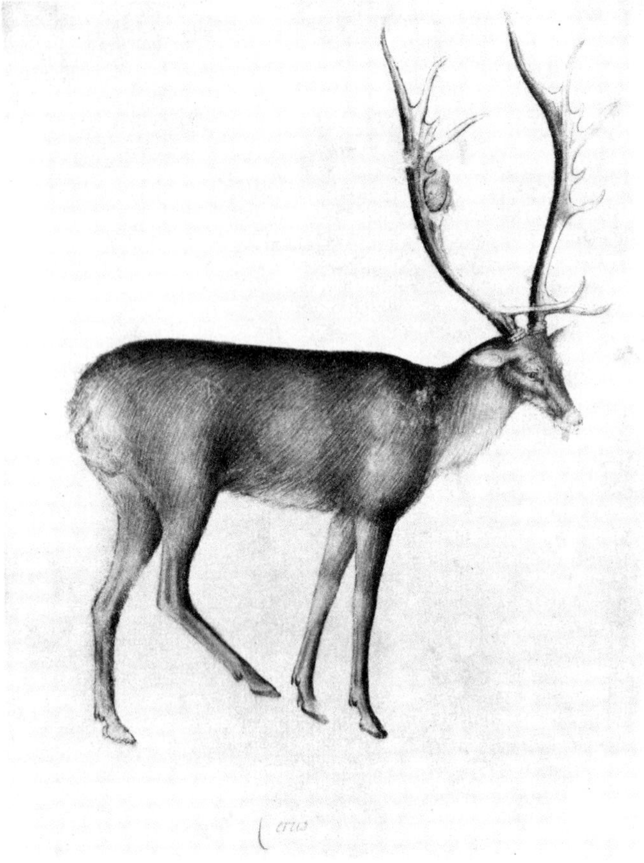
PLATE 14

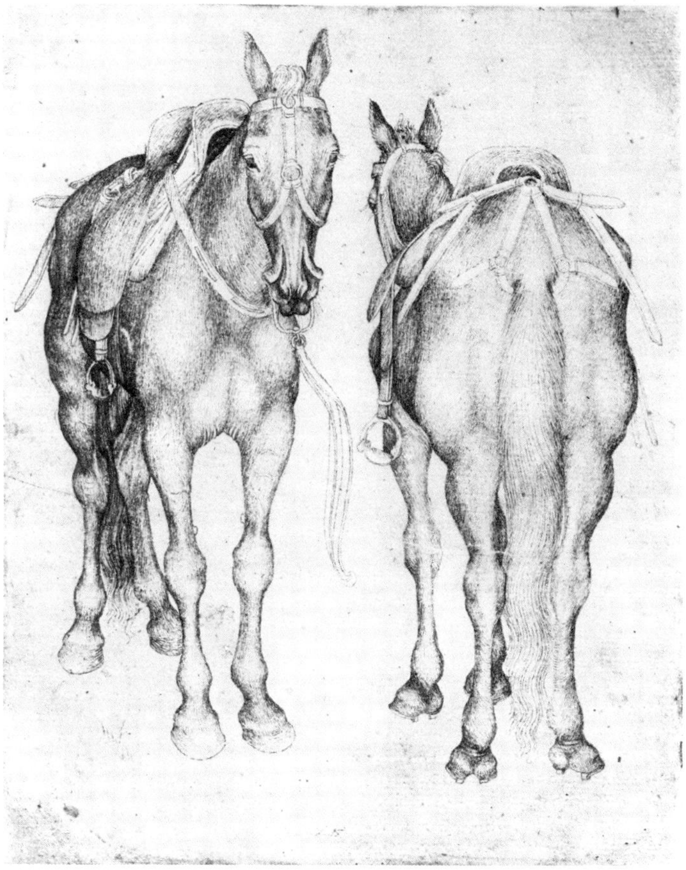
PLATE 15

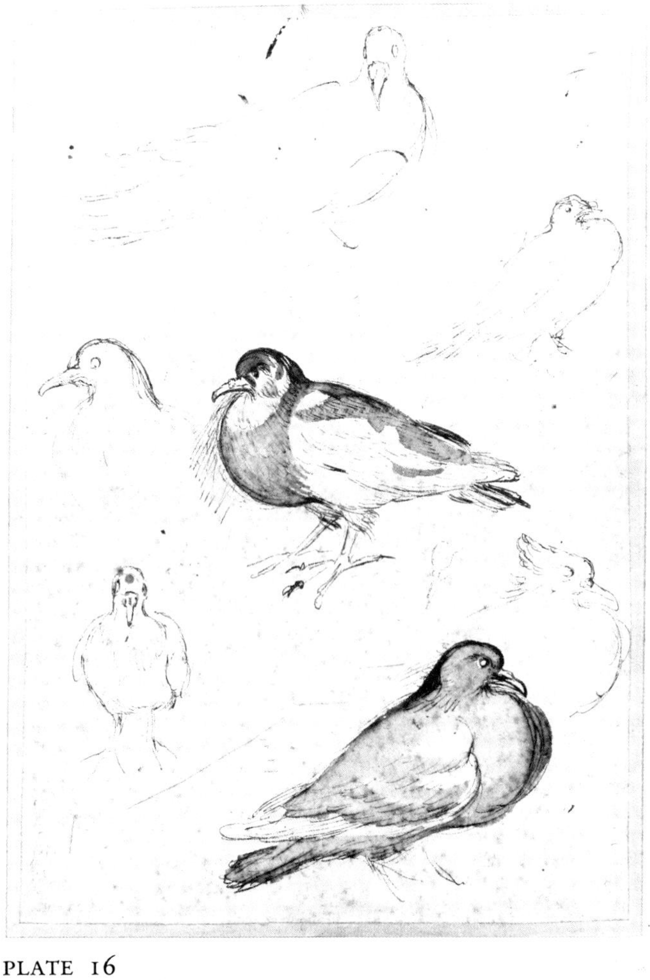
PLATE 16

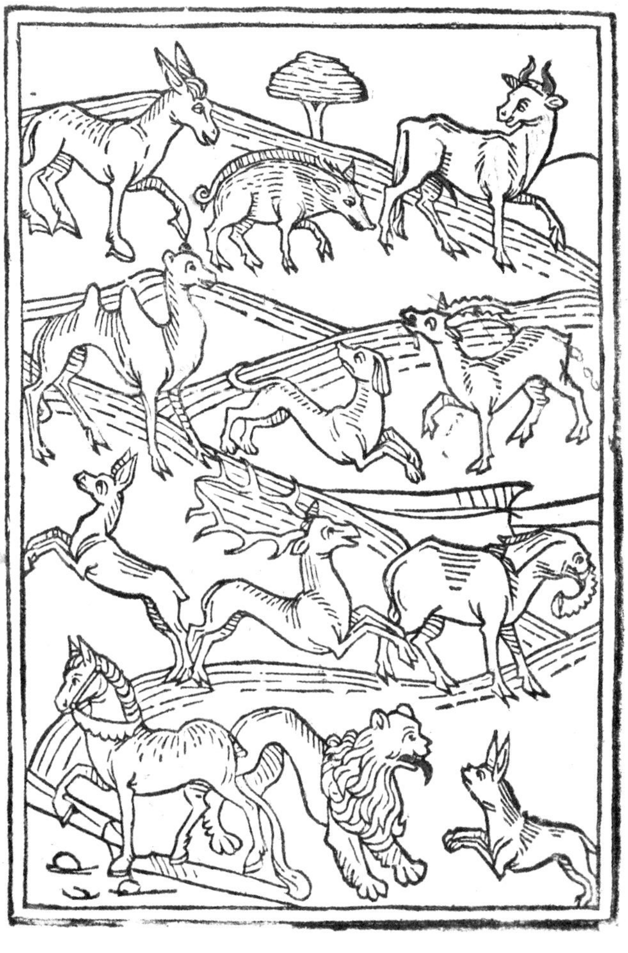
PLATE 17

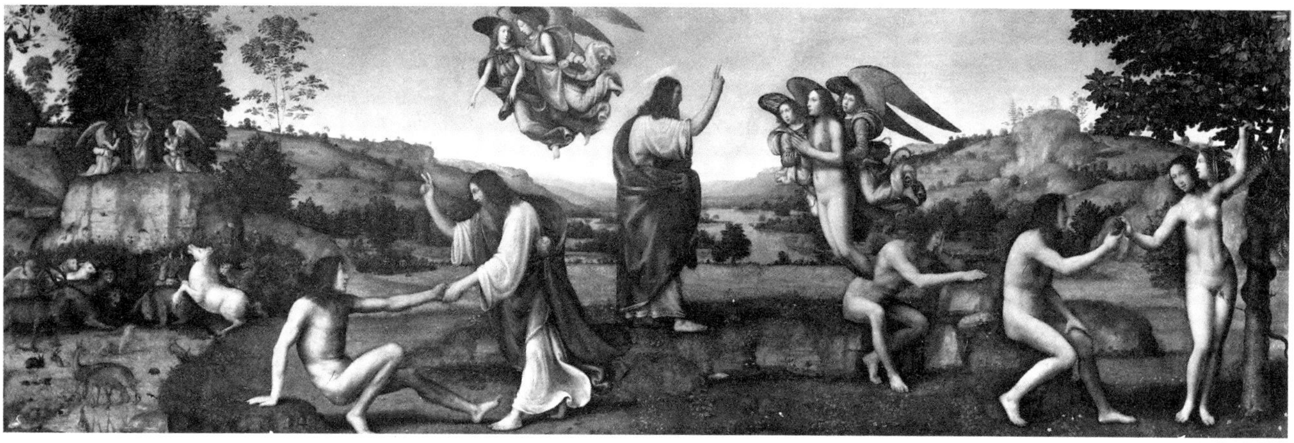

PLATE 18

THE ANIMALS

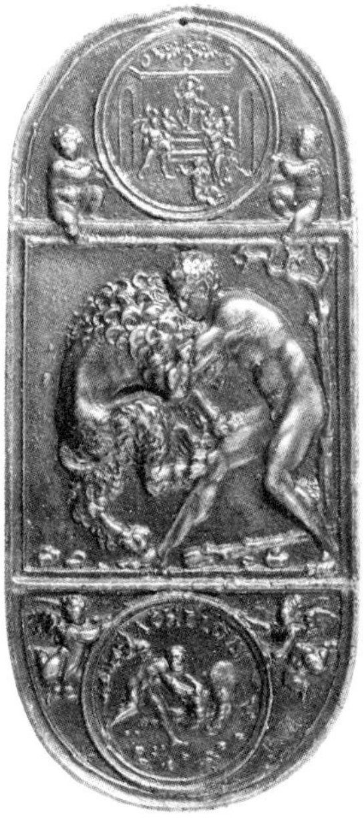

PLATE 19

A deer, a hyena, a bear, a bull and numerous birds are among the many creatures that can be identified in *The Forest Fire*. The variety of animal life depicted in the picture attests Piero di Cosimo's zoological interests mentioned by Vasari. However, such a fascination for natural species was not an exception in the fifteenth century, especially in those works of art connected with court life and executed in the International Gothic style, although it is difficult to find many paintings in this tradition where animals are treated as the main theme. A rare example is that cited by Vasari of Pesellino's animal pictures once in the Palazzo Medici, Florence, and now lost.

It is impossible to know exactly how many animals Piero di Cosimo or other artists of that time were able to observe at first hand. Vasari says that he had a sketch book of animal studies and this may have contained sheets like the famous and very closely observed studies by the Lombard painter Giovanni de' Grassi (PLATE 14) or Pisanello (PLATE 15), or by later artists such as those once associated with Giovanni da Udine (PLATE 16). By the late fifteenth century printed books containing drawings of animals (PLATE 17) became available of which artists could have made use when called upon to treat subjects as diverse as scenes from Genesis (PLATE 18), the labours of Hercules (PLATE 19), the legend of Orpheus (PLATE 20) or the poetry of Dante (PLATE 21).

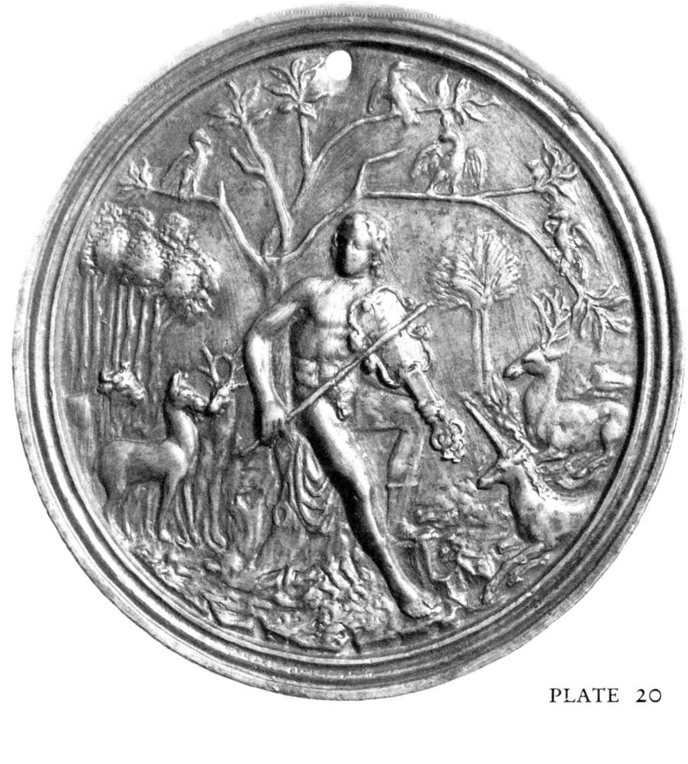

PLATE 20

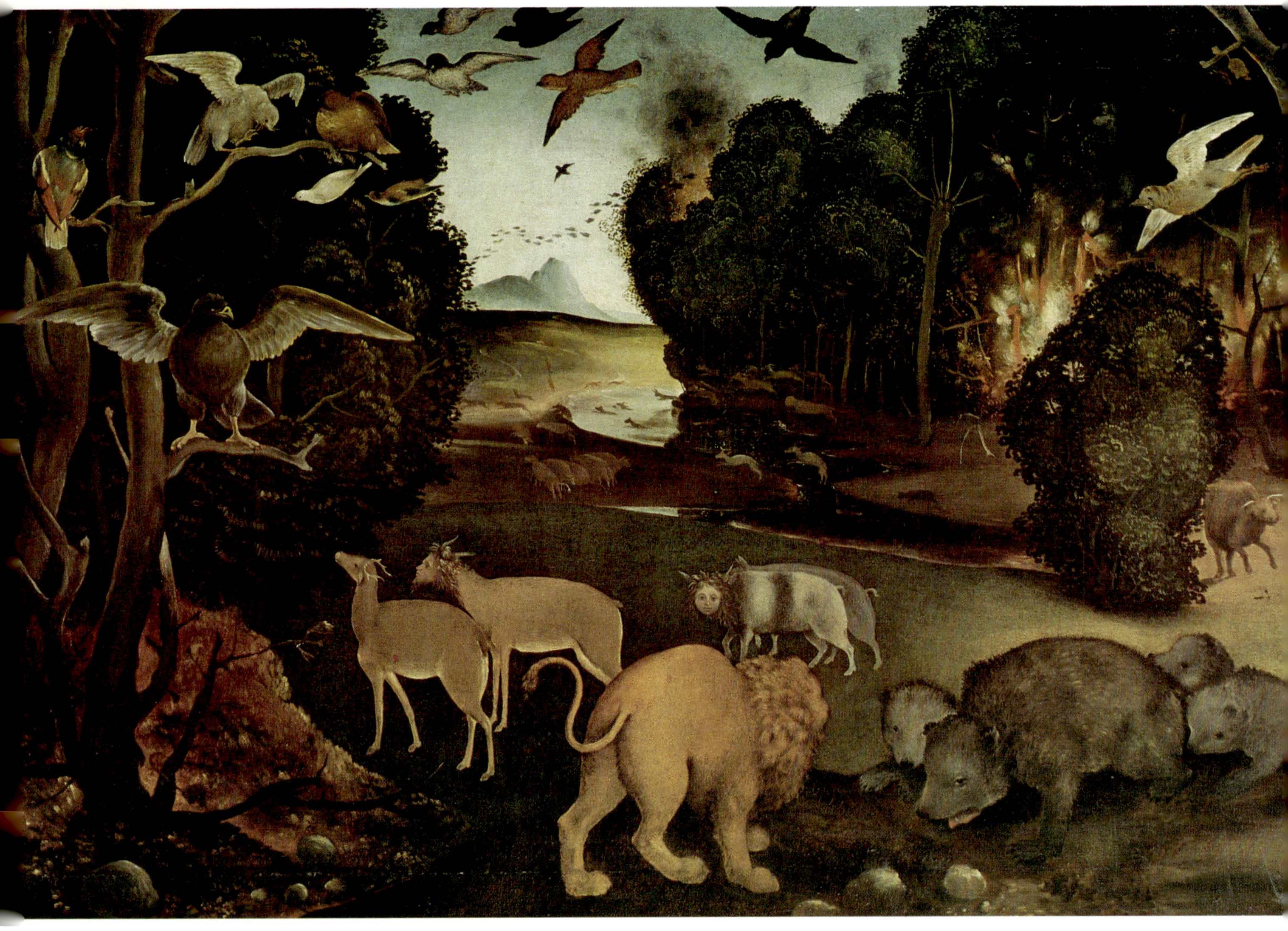

THE FOREST FIRE

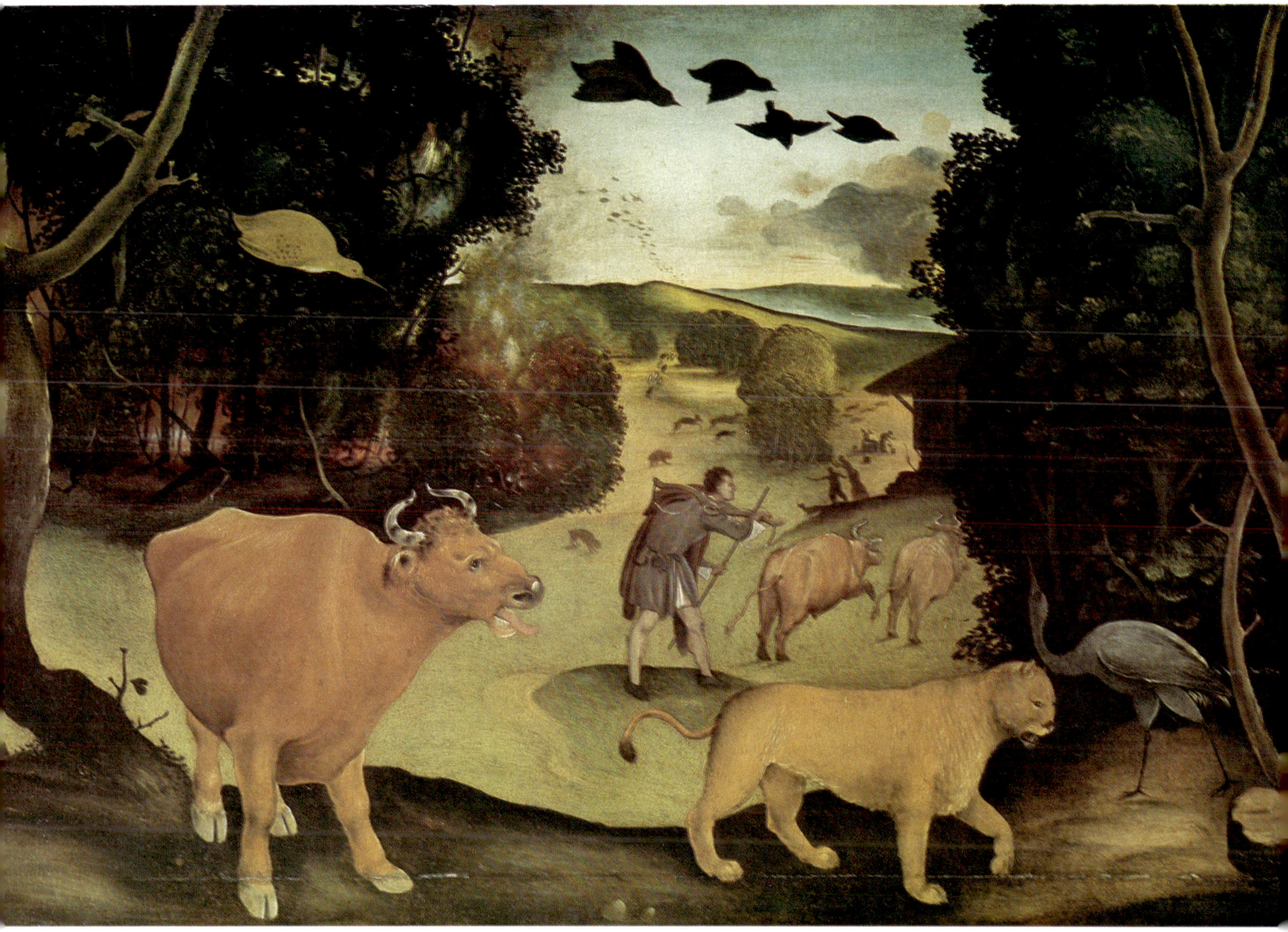

PIERO DI COSIMO

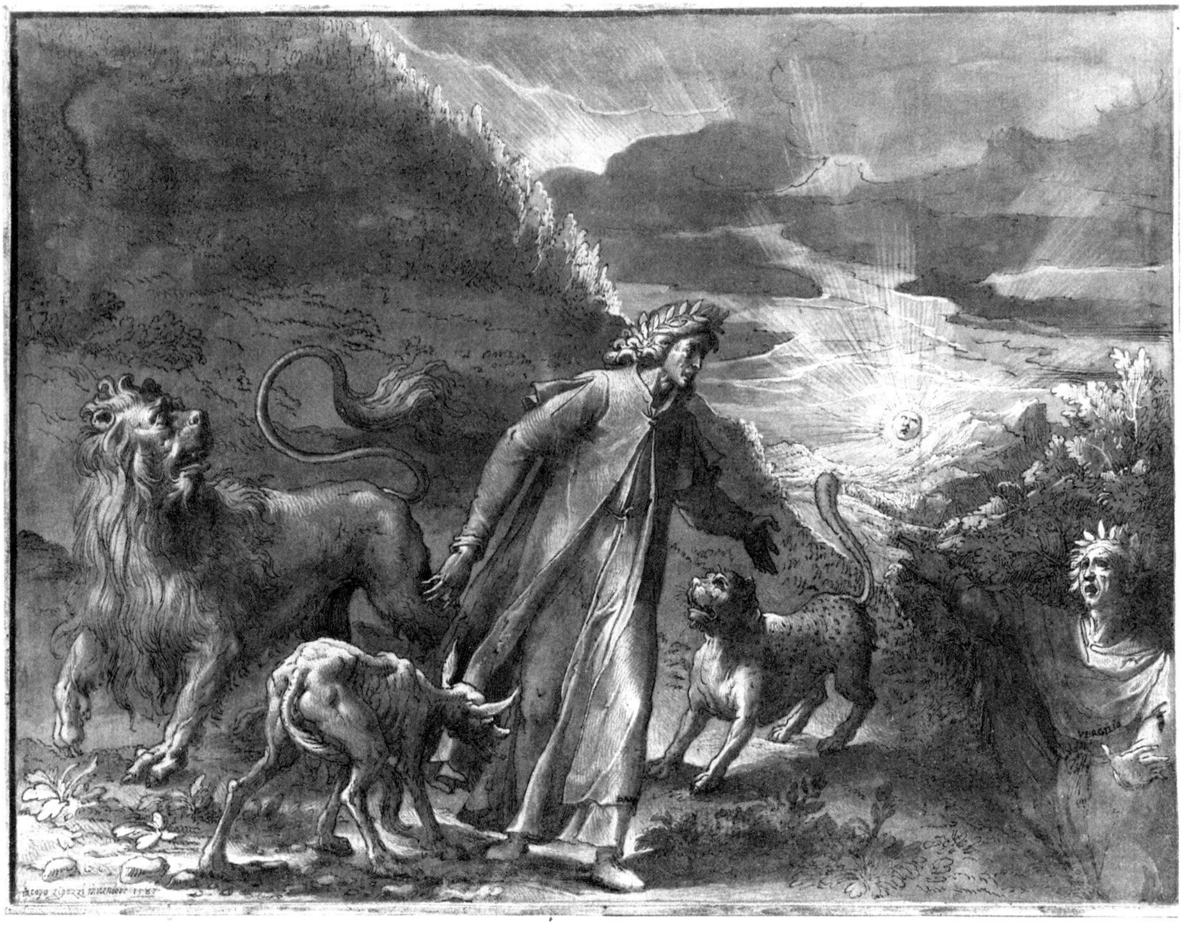

PLATE 21

PLATE 23

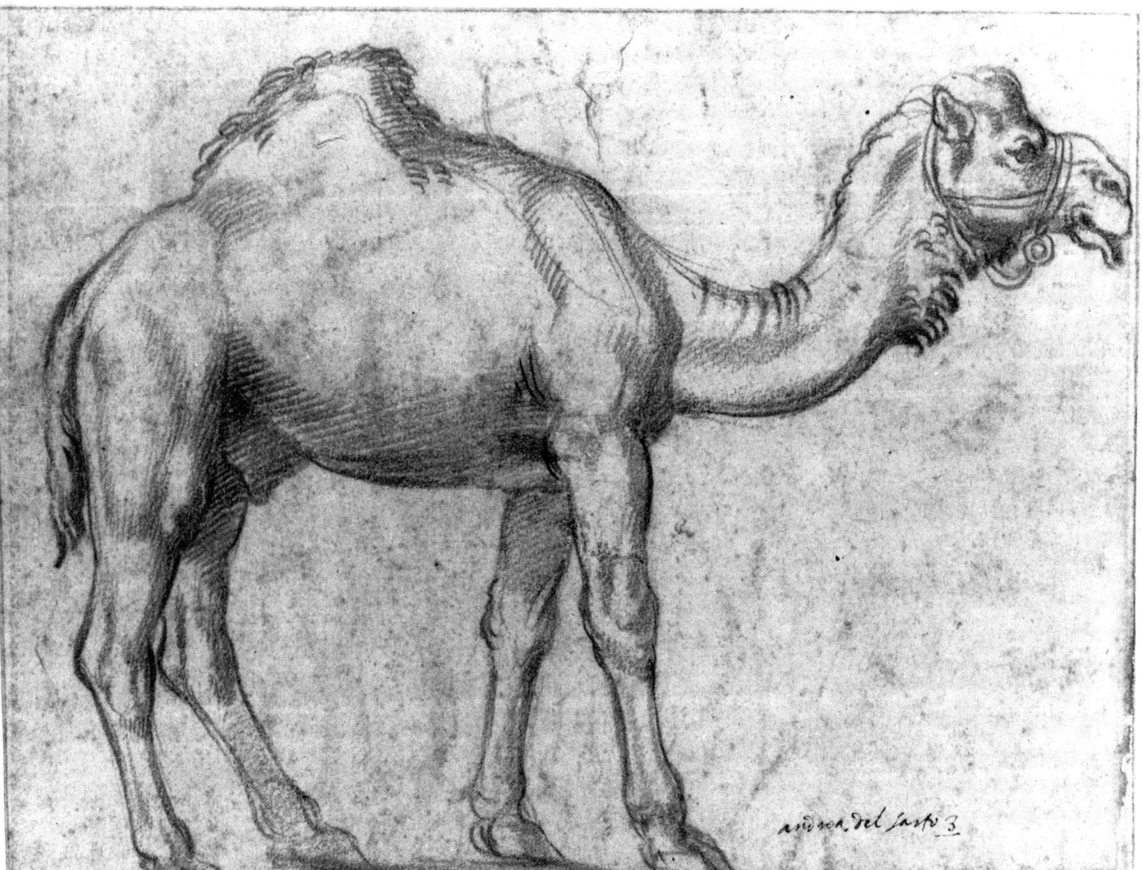

There had also been a steady flow of live exotic animals into Europe since the Middle Ages as a result of presentations or diplomatic gifts, and many Renaissance rulers established menageries. Those of Réné, Count of Anjou and Provence, who later became King of the Sicilies, and Pope Leo X (PLATE 22) were particularly famous. Often travellers returned to Europe with animals acquired in the Levant (PLATE 23), and in many Italian cities during the fifteenth and sixteenth centuries combats of wild animals were sometimes specially staged (PLATE 24) as a sport for spectators. A description of one of these held in 1514 is given by the Florentine diarist Luca Landucci:

'25th June. There was a hunt in the *Piazza de' Signori*: two lions, and bears, leopards, bulls, buffaloes, stags and many other wild animals of various kinds, and horses; the lions were brought in after the rest, and chiefly the one that came first did nothing, on account of the great tumult of the crowd; except that certain big dogs approaching him, he siezed one with his paw and dropped it dead on the ground, and a second the same, without taking any notice of

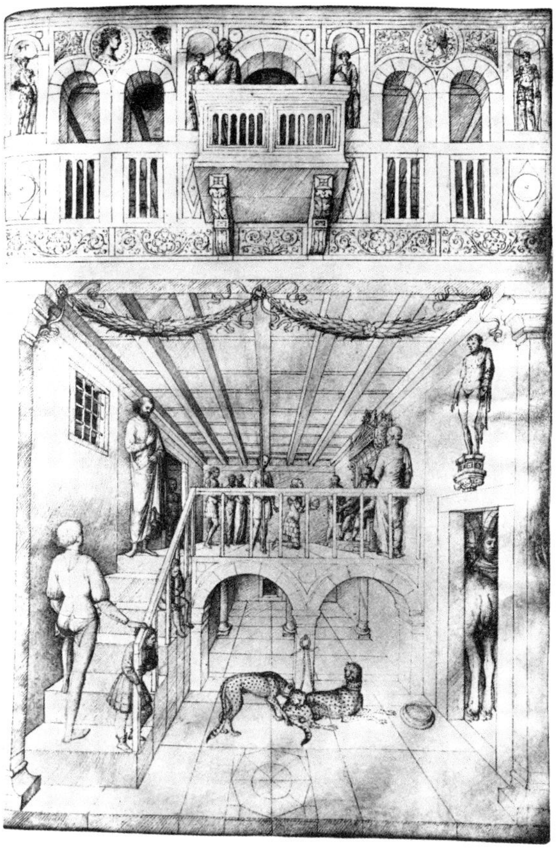

PLATE 22

PLATE 24

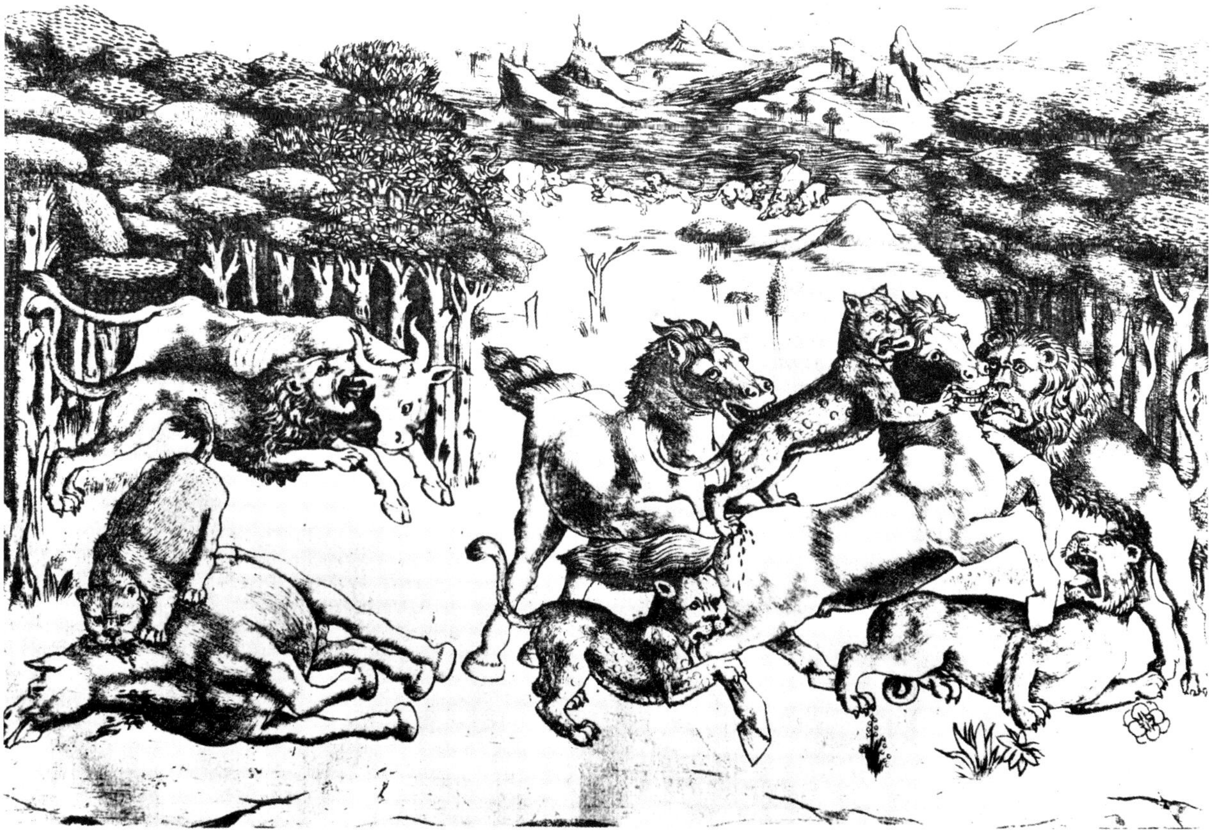

the other wild beasts: when he was not molested, he stood quite still, and then went away further on. They had made a tortoise and a porcupine, inside of which were men who made them move along on wheels all over the Piazza, and kept thrusting at the animals with their lances. This hunt was thought so much of, that the number of wooden platforms and enclosures made in the Piazza was a thing never before seen, the cost of bringing the timber and of erecting these stands being very great; it seemed incredible that any city in the world could have such a mass of timber One carpenter paid 40 gold florins for the permission to put up a platform against one of these houses, and there were people who paid three or four *grossoni* for a place on the stands. All the stands and enclosures were crowded, as also the windows and the roofs such a concourse of people never having been known, for numbers of strangers had come from may different parts. . . . At the end of the evening it was found that many men had been injured and about three killed in fighting with the wild beasts; one had been killed by a buffalo. They had made a beautiful large fountain in the middle of the Piazza, which threw the water up in four jets, and round this fountain was a wood of verdure with certain dens very convenient for the animals to hide in, and low troughs full of water round the fountain for them to be able to drink. . . . Finally the lions made no more attacks, becoming cowed by the immense tumult of the people.'

Some of these animals gained considerable reputations in their own right and were often drawn by artists. Famous examples are Raphael's drawing of the elephant Hanno (PLATE 25), or Dürer's woodcut of the rhinoceros (PLATE 26). An example of a popular diplomatic gift is the giraffe which can be seen on the right of the painting *Vulcan and Aeolus* (PLATE 12), and was probably the giraffe sent to Lorenzo de' Medici from Egypt in 1487, which was described in a lengthy account (11-25 November) by Landucci as 'A very tall giraffe, beautiful and graceful', and engraved and painted well into the sixteenth century (PLATE 27).

An alternative source for Piero di Cosimo was the written accounts of animals recorded by travellers, such as Breydenbach, *Peregrinatio ad Terram Sanctam* (1486) (PLATE 28). Yet, although the earliest printed zoological works date from the fifteenth century, the principal compendiums were not compiled until the sixteenth and seventeenth centuries. These were clearly not available for Piero di Cosimo to consult, but, the main sources, namely Ctesias's *Persica and Indica*, Aristotle's *Historia Animalium*, Pliny the Elder's *Naturalis Historia* and Aelian's *De Natura Animalium*, might have been known to him. It might, in fact, have been from such written sources, or from the theory of evolution propounded by Lucretius in *De rerum natura* (Book V, 821-924), that the artist derived the idea of showing quadrupeds with human faces, since such creatures are described by Ctesias, writing in the fifth century B.C., and by Aelian writing in the second and third centuries A.D. So strong was the dependence on this particular literary tradition that the sixteenth century cosmographer Andre Thévet illustrated such an

PLATE 25

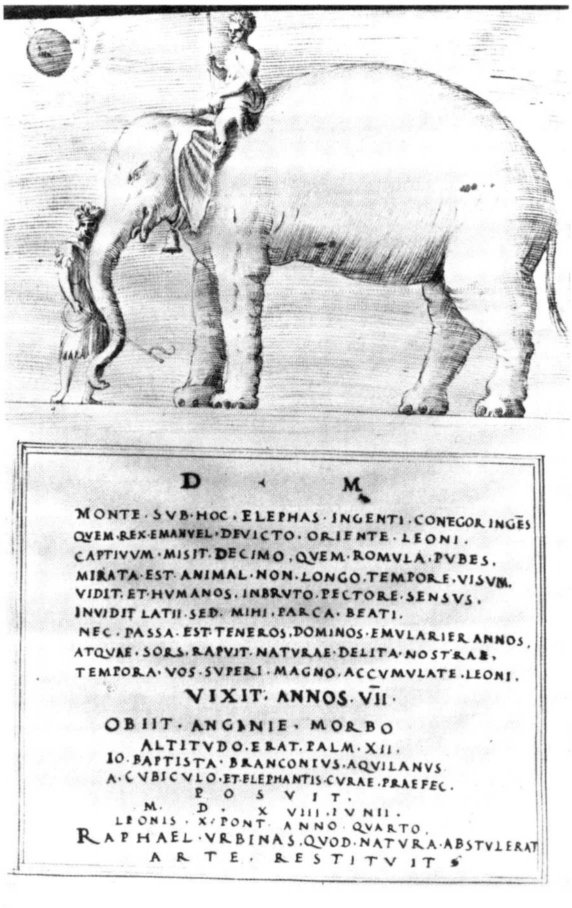

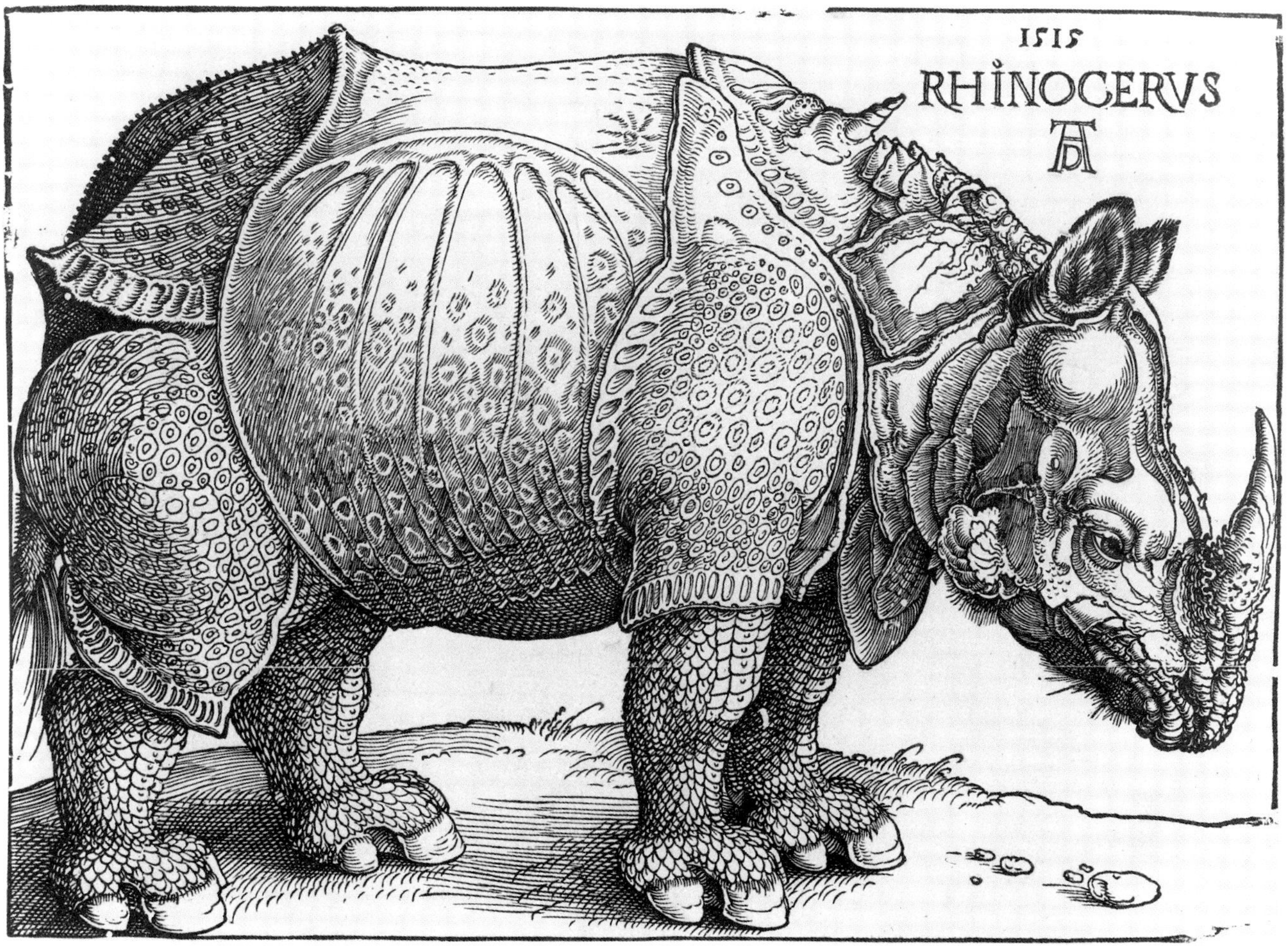

PLATE 26

PLATE 27

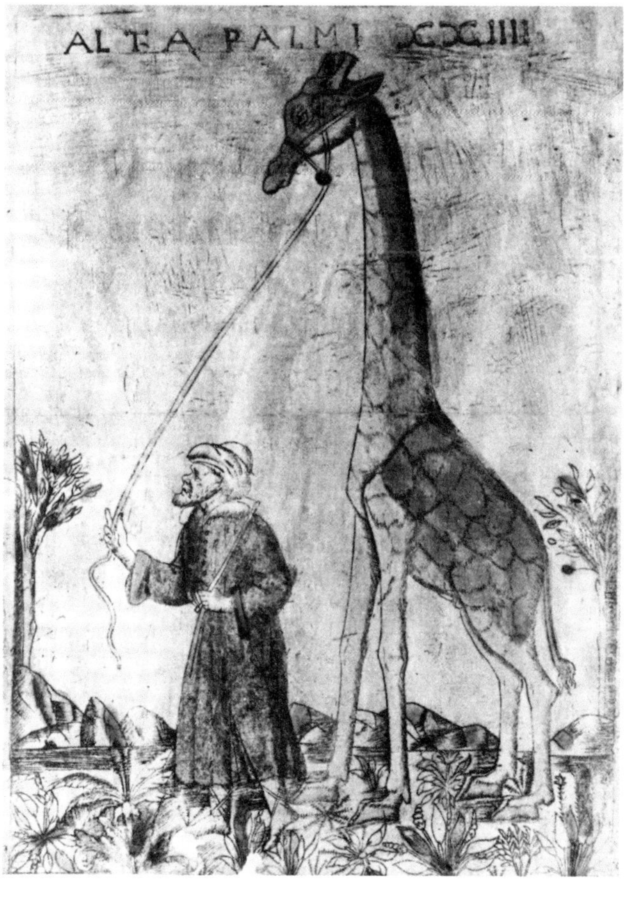

PLATE 28

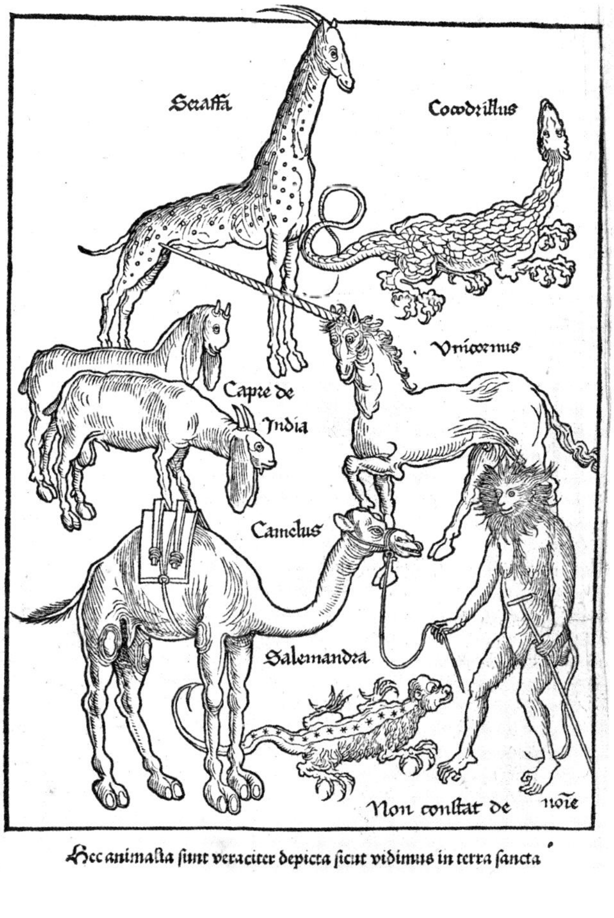

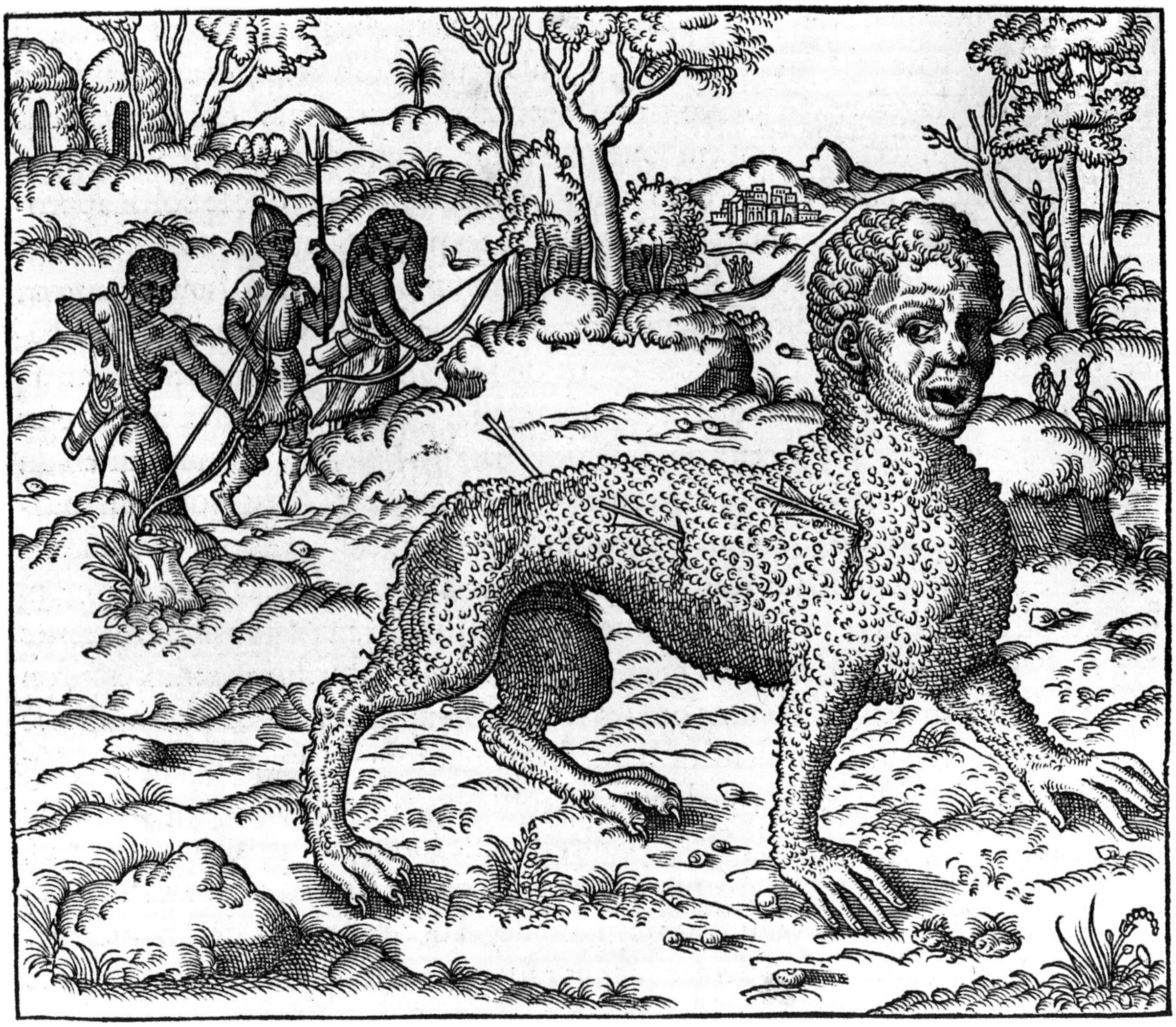

PLATE 29

PLATE 30

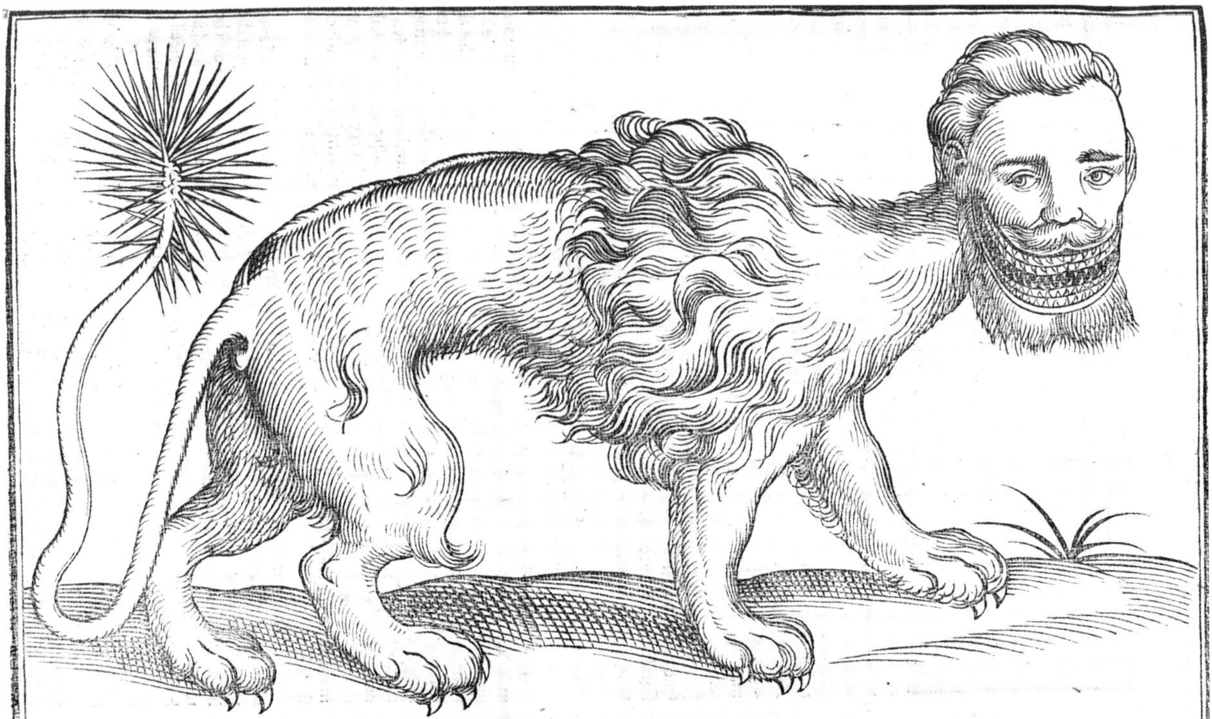

animal in his *La Cosmographie universelle* (1571) (PLATE 29) claiming that it could still actually be seen along the banks of the Red Sea. This animal is again illustrated in the first English edition (1607) of Conrad Gesner's famous book, *Historiae Animalium*, issued by Edward Topsell with the title *The Historie of the Foure-footed Beastes: collected out of all the volumes of Conrad Gesner . . .* (PLATE 30). There the quadruped with a human face is described as a breed of hyena known as the mantichora (from the Persian meaning 'man eater'), which was believed to be endowed with the body of a tiger, the tail of a scorpion and the face of a human. For the treatment of birds, reference to Pierre Belon's *L'Histoire de la Nature des Oiseaux* (1555) is helpful because most of the birds depicted in *The Forest Fire* are reproduced, often in diagrams based on dissections. Comparison with Belon's book, however, helps to place the picture in its proper context as an imaginative recreation of primitive life as opposed to a scientific, or quasi-scientific, treatise.

On a wider basis 'animal portraiture' had connotations of a more specific kind. The tradition of imbuing animals with a particular symbolical significance was most marked in the Middle Ages. Medieval bestiaries, which were collections of articles on animals alluding to their habits as exemplifications of moral and religious behaviour (PLATE 31), are symptomatic of this development. Animal symbolism continued in the Renaissance as emblemata often reproduced in the form of plaquettes and medals (PLATE 32), although this particular interpretation is not relevant in the context of *The Forest Fire*. However, another aspect of Renaissance thought combining both the zoological and the emblematic strands does occur in *The Forest Fire*. This is the Renaissance attitude to physiognomy, where human characteristics are equated with animal features in the sense that the figures in the equestrian monuments by Donatello, Verrocchio or Leonardo da Vinci are given leonine features to signify their prowess as soldiers or leaders. It is unlikely that analysis of the animals in *The Forest Fire* will reveal any hidden meanings, but in a general sense the relationship between man and animals would not have been missed by the Renaissance viewer.

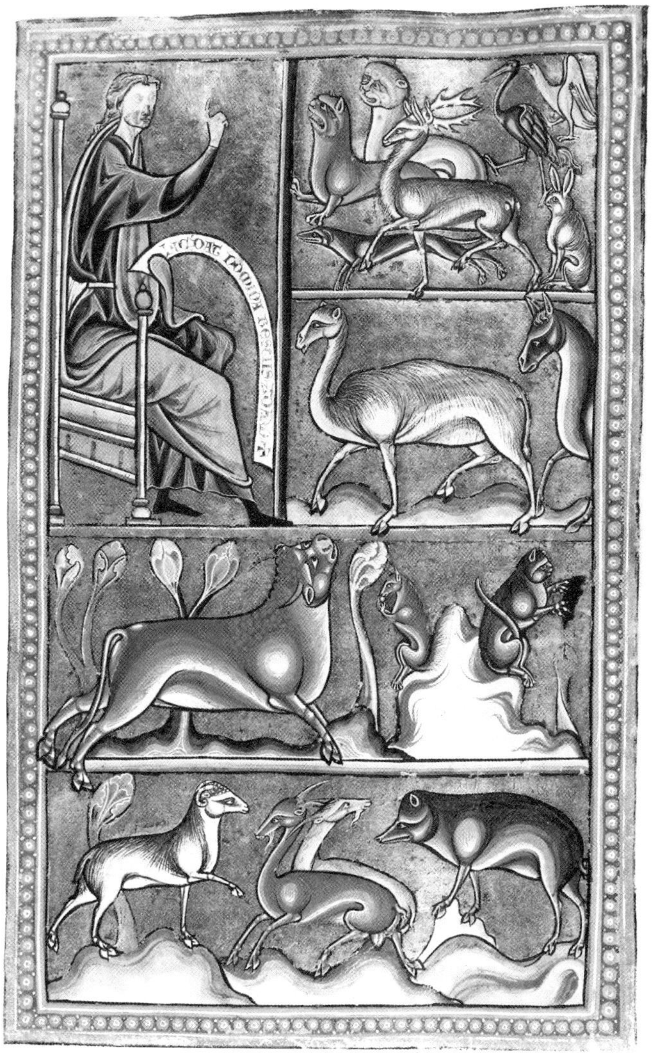

PLATE 31

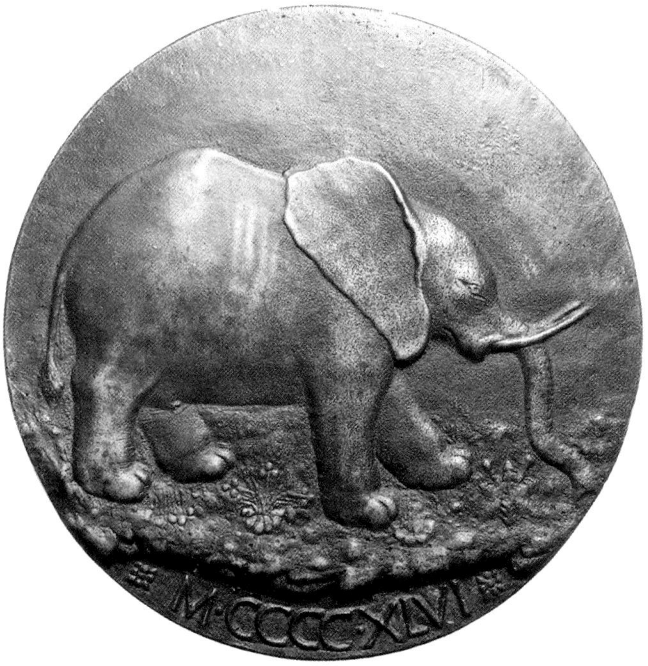

PLATE 32

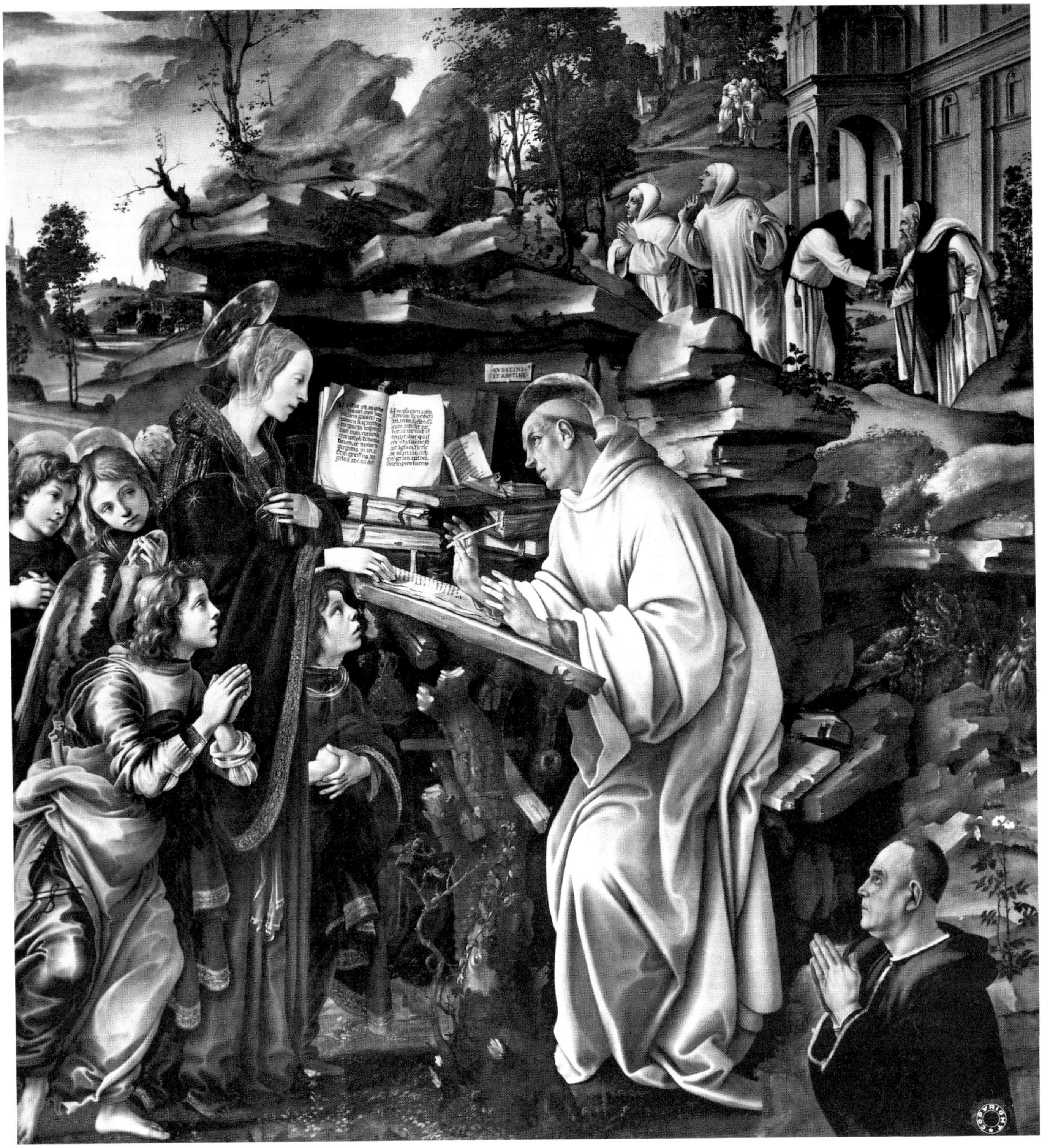

PLATE 33

THE PATRON

PIERO di Cosimo, despite his eccentric habits, was a highly regarded and widely patronised artist in Florence. The Pugliese family, for example, commissioned several works from him and had been leading patrons in Florence for at least a century. An earlier member of the family commissioned the important frescoes (now lost) by Starnina in the chapel of St. Jerome in the church of St. Maria del Carmine, Florence, and subsequently during the course of the fifteenth century, they continued to patronise the city's chief artists. The Pugliese derived their wealth from wool, Florence's main trade during the fourteenth and fifteenth centuries.

Piero di Cosimo's series of pictures illustrating the history of primordial man was connected by Panofsky with the following passage in Vasari's *Life* referring to the Pugliese family:

'Around a chamber in the house of Francesco del Pugliese, Piero painted historical events . . . the figures being small. In this work also the artist has exhibited a singular variety of those fantastic objects which he so greatly delighted in painting; the buildings, the animals, the vestments, the instruments, all are of the most fanciful and varied character, he depicted whatever came into his head in short, the whole representation being entirely fabulous. After the death of Francesco del Pugliese and his sons, these paintings were removed, nor do I know what became of them. A similar fate has befallen a picture of Mars and Venus, with Cupids and Vulcan, a work exhibiting evidence of consummate art, and finished with wonderful patience.'[2]

Two members of the Pugliese family came into contact with Piero di Cosimo. Firstly, Piero di Francesco del Pugliese, who held several important positions in Florentine life, including Prior in 1475 and *gonfaloniere* in 1480. Secondly, Piero di Francesco's nephew, Francesco di Filippo di Francesco del Pugliese, who was born in 1458, and later shared a house with his uncle. Francesco also held public office being Prior in 1491 and again in 1497. He was, however, an ardent supporter of Savonarola and was exiled from Florence on the return of the Medici in 1512; he died in 1519. Between them they were responsible for commissioning and collecting a considerable number of important works of art. As has been mentioned, Piero di

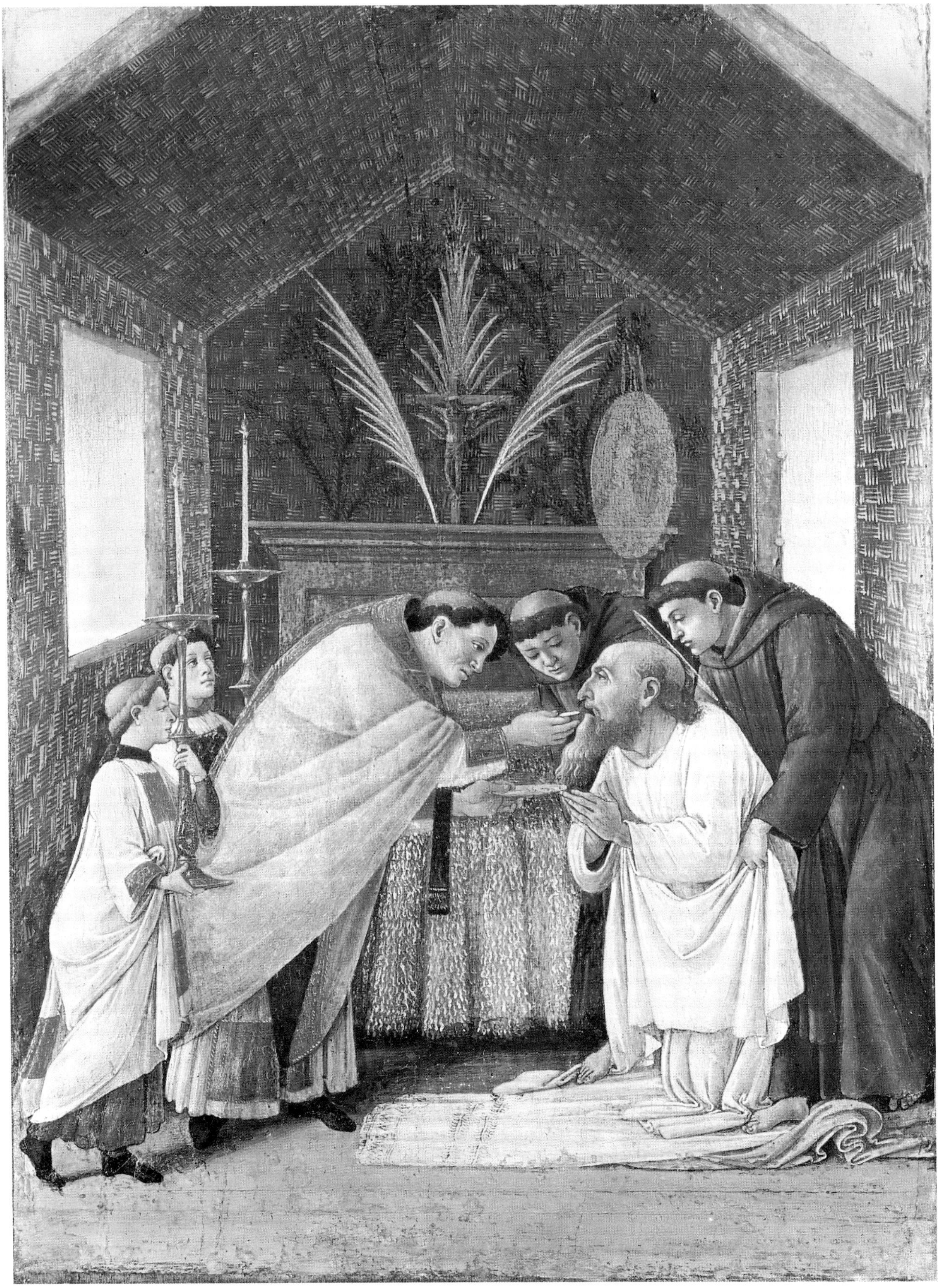

Francesco commissioned two altarpieces from Piero di Cosimo, *Virgin and Child with Saints Peter, John the Baptist, Nicholas of Bari and Dominic* (PLATE 2) and *Virgin and Child with Saints Catherine of Alexandria, Rosa of Viterbo, Peter and John the Evangelist* (PLATE 5) and he also commissioned *The Vision of Saint Bernardino* by Filippino Lippi (PLATE 33) (now in the Badia, Florence) in which the figure of the donor is possibly a portrait. The family also commissioned works from Antonio Pollaiuolo, Fra Bartolommeo, Raffaellino del Garbo, and Botticelli (*The Last Communion of Saint Jerome*, PLATE 34). The Pugliese also owned works by Fra Angelico and Donatello (*The Quincy Shaw Madonna*, PLATE 35). As patrons, therefore, the Pugliese showed considerable discernment.

The Forest Fire may well have been one of the paintings seen by Vasari in the Pugliese household, as suggested by Panofsky, but there is some doubt now as to whether the whole of the elaborate and learned reconstruction put upon the passage quoted above is really valid. Although *The Forest Fire* is slightly longer than the two panels in New York, there is a certain compatability in the subject-matter and style. Yet, the pictures in Hartford and Ottawa are painted on canvas and have a vertical format, being conceived on a different scale. Such differences, Panofsky argued, could have been dictated by the proportions of the room, or rooms, in which the pictures were distributed, but this seems unlikely and in any case Vasari's account does not actually describe the pictures in the Pugliese household as belonging to a single sequence. Indeed, as expressed by Vasari, the implication is that the paintings of *Mars and Venus* and *Vulcan* (presumably PLATE 11) were quite separate from those mentioned at the beginning of the quotation.

The Forest Fire seems to have disappeared after leaving the possession of the Pugliese family and it only appears again, as far as is known, towards the end of the nineteenth century when it was in the collection of the Rucellai family in Florence. The painting was bought from the Rucellai family towards the end of the First World War by Prince Paul of Yugoslavia and it was presented by the National Art-Collections Fund to The Ashmolean Museum in 1933, when Kenneth Clark was keeper of the Department of Art, as it was then known.

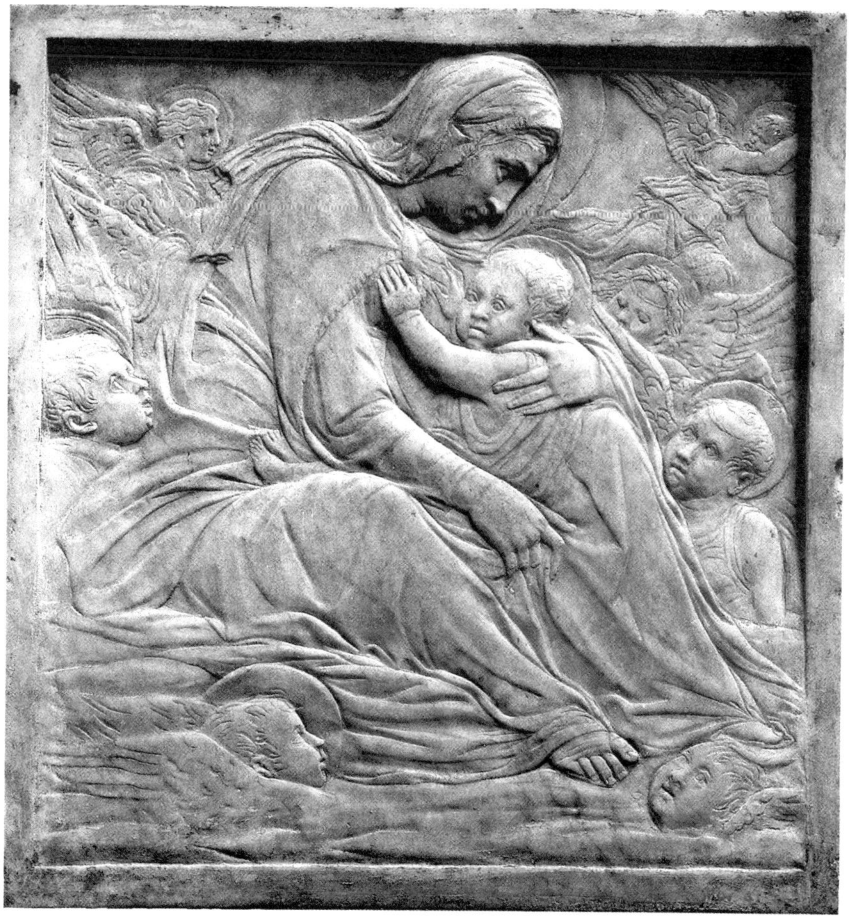

PLATE 34

PLATE 35

ILLUSTRATIONS

CENTRE PAGE
The Forest Fire Piero di Cosimo. c.1505. Panel. 71.2×202cm. Ashmolean Museum, Oxford.

PLATE 1
Portrait of Piero di Cosimo Cristoforo Coriolano. Woodcut. From the second edition of Vasari's *Lives of the Artists* Florence, 1568; headpiece to the *Life of Piero di Cosimo*

PLATE 2
Altarpiece (Virgin and Child with Saints Peter, John the Baptist, Nicholas of Bari and Dominic) Piero di Cosimo. c.1485-90. Panel. 166.5×113cm. St. Louis City Art Gallery, Missouri. Painted for the Pugliese chapel in St. Spirito, Florence.

PLATE 3
The Visitation with Saints Nicholas of Bari and Anthony Abbot Piero di Cosimo. c.1485-90. Panel. 184×189cm. National Gallery of Art, Washington (Kress Collection). Painted for the chapel of Gino Capponi in St. Spirito, Florence.

PLATE 4
The Portinari Altarpiece Hugo Van Der Goes. 1483. Panel. 253×586cm. Uffizi, Florence. Painted for the hospital church of St. Maria Nuova, Florence.

PLATE 5
Altarpiece (Virgin and Child with Saints Catherine of Alexandria, Rosa of Viterbo, Peter and John the Evangelist) Piero di Cosimo. c.1495-1500. Panel. 203×197cm. Ospedale degli Innocenti, Florence. Commissioned by Piero di Francesco Pugliese.

PLATE 6
Virgin and Child with Angels Piero di Cosimo. c.1510. Panel. 116×85cm. Cini collection, Venice.

PLATE 7
The Death of Procris Piero di Cosimo. c.1500. Panel. 65×183cm. National Gallery, London.

PLATE 8
The Battle of Lapiths and Centaurs Piero di Cosimo. c.1505. Panel. 71×260cm. National Gallery, London

PLATE 9
The Hunt Piero di Cosimo. c.1505. Panel. 70.5×169cm. The Metropolitan Museum, New York.

PLATE 10
The Return from the Hunt Piero di Cosimo. c.1505. Panel. 70.5×168.9cm. The Metropolitan Museum, New York.

PLATE 11
The Finding of Vulcan on Lemnos Piero di Cosimo. 1505-10. Canvas. 155.6×174cm. Wadsworth Athenaeum, Hartford, Connecticut.

PLATE 12
Vulcan and Aeolus Piero di Cosimo. 1505-10. Canvas. 156×165cm. National Gallery of Canada, Ottawa.

PLATE 13
The Discovery of Fire Woodcut. From Vitruvius' *De Architectura* Book II, 1511.

PLATE 14
Study of a Deer Giovanni de' Grassi. 14th century. Drawing. 26×17.5cm. Accademia Carrara, Bergamo.

PLATE 15
Studies of a Horse Pisanello. c.1444. Drawing. 269mm×168mm. Musée du Louvre, Paris.

PLATE 16
Studies of Pigeons Ascribed to Giovanni da Udine. (1487-1561 or 1564). Drawing. 252×175mm. Christ Church Picture Gallery, Oxford.

PLATE 17
Page from Das Buch der Natur Woodcut. From K. Von Megenberg, *Das Buch der Natur*, 1481. Bodleian Library, Oxford.

PLATE 18
The Creation Mariotto Albertinelli. c.1520. Panel. 56.5×165.5mm. University of London, Courtauld Institute Galleries.

PLATE 19
Hercules and the Nemean Lion Moderno. c.1500. Bronze plaquette. 75×56.25mm. Ashmolean Museum, Oxford.

PLATE 20
Orpheus Moderno. c.1500. Bronze plaquette. Diameter 103mm. Ashmolean Museum, Oxford.

PLATE 21
Dante surrounded by the three beasts and Virgil appearing to Dante Jacopo Lizozzi. 1587. Drawing. 205×278mm. Christ Church Picture Gallery, Oxford.

PLATE 22
The Head of Hannibal presented to Prusias Jacopo Bellini. c.1450. Drawing. 427×290mm. From Jacopo Bellini's sketchbook divided between London (British Museum) and Paris (Musée du Louvre). This sheet is from the part in Paris (f.XL) and is an imaginary scene showing leopards kept as pets in the courtyard of a palace, reflecting contemporary practice in fifteenth century Italy. Several of the drawings in Jacopo Bellini's sketchbook are studies of individual animals or groups of animals fighting as in Plate 24.

PLATE 23
Study of a Camel Ascribed to Bandinelli (1493-1560). Drawing. 230×300mm. Christ Church Picture Gallery, Oxford.

PLATE 24
Wild Animals attacking Horses and Oxen Engraving. Florentine c.1460. 184×252mm. British Museum, London.

PLATE 25
Hanno; the elephant Francisco D'Ollandia after Raphael c.1539-40. 460×350mm. Escorial, Madrid. The elephant was sent as a gift to Leo X by King Emmanual of Portugal in 1514, together with leopards and ostriches and other beasts. When the elephant died in 1516 Leo X was so distressed that he commissioned Raphael to design a monument in its memory. This drawing is of Raphael's monument which no longer survives.

PLATE 26
Rhinoceros Albrecht Dürer. 1515. Woodcut. 212×300mm. Oxford, Ashmolean Museum.

PLATE 27
Giraffe 1470-90. Engraving. 258×183mm. Inserted into a manuscript copy of Sigismondo Tizio, *Historiae Seneses* in the Biblioteca Vaticana, Rome. Honoured by poets and artists the giraffe survived for many years in Florence. It is represented in a famous fifteenth century manuscript known as the Codex Ashmoleansis now in the Bodleian Library, Oxford. (Lat.misc. d.85 ff.LXXIIv. and LXXIIIr. Vasari painted the scene of *Lorenzo de' Medici receiving the Ambassadors from Egypt*, which includes the giraffe, as a fresco in the Palazzo Vecchio, Florence.

PLATE 28
Page from Peregrinatio ad Terram Sanctam Woodcut. From B. von Breydenbach, *Peregrinatio ad Terram Sanctam*, 1486. Bodleian Library, Oxford.

PLATE 29
Page from La Cosmographie Universelle Engraving. From André Thevet, *La Cosmographie Universelle*, 1571. Bodleian Library, Oxford.

PLATE 30
Page from The Historie of the Foure-footed Beastes . . . Engraving. From E. Topsell, *The Historie of the Foure-footed Beastes: collected out of all the volumes of Conrad Gesner . . .*, 1607. Bodleian Library, Oxford.

PLATE 31
Page from an English Bestiary Peterborough. Thirteenth century. Bodleian Library, Oxford. This manuscript was once owned by the Tradescants and by Elias Ashmole, the founder of the Ashmolean Museum.

PLATE 32
Reverse of a medal of Isotta Malatesta Matteo de' Pasti. 1441-67. Bronze. Diameter 84mm. Ashmolean Museum, Oxford.

PLATE 33
The Vision of St. Bernardino Filippino Lippi. c.1490. Panel. Badia, Florence.

PLATE 34
The Last Communion of St. Jerome Sandro Botticelli. c.1490. Panel. 340×255mm. The Metropolitan Museum, New York.

PLATE 35
Virgin and Child (Quincy Shaw Madonna) Donatello. c.1425-8. Marble. 335×320mm. Museum of Fine Arts, Boston.

SELECTED BIBLIOGRAPHY

THE ARTIST AND HIS STYLE

R. L. DOUGLAS, *Piero di Cosimo* (Chicago, 1946)
R. and M. WITTKOWKER, *Born under Saturn* (London, 1963)
M. BACCI, *Piero di Cosimo* (Milan, 1966)
G. VASARI, *Lives of the Most excellent Painters, Sculptors and Architects* (1568) translated by Mrs J. Foster (London, 1855-64)
H. W. JANSON, 'The "Image Made by Chance" in Renaissance Thought' reprinted in *16 Studies* (New York, n.d.), pp.53-74.

THE PICTURE AND ITS SUBJECT

SIR J. G. FRAZER, *The Myths of the Origin of Fire* (London, 1930)
E. PANOFSKY, *Studies in Iconology* (Oxford and New York, 1962) first published as 'The Early History of Man in a Series of Paintings by Piero di Cosimo', *Journal of the Warburg Institute*, I (1937-8)
A. R. TURNER, *The Vision of Landscape in Renaissance Italy* (Princeton, 1966)
C. LLOYD, *A Catalogue of the Earlier Italian Paintings in The Ashmolean Museum* (Oxford, 1977)
L. SILVER, "Forest Primeval: Albrecht Altdorfer and the German Wilderness Landscape", *Simiolus Netherlands Quarterly for the History of Art*, 13 (1983), pp.5-43.
K CHRISTIANSEN, 'Early Renaissance Narrative Painting in Italy', *The Metropolitan Museum of Art Bulletin* (Fall, 1983), pp.38-47.

THE ANIMALS

J. BARCLAY LLOYD, *African Animals in Renaissance Literature and Art* (Oxford, 1971)
K. CLARK, *Animals and Man* (London, 1977)
K. THOMAS, *Man and the Natural World* (London, 1983)

THE PATRON

H. HORNE, 'The Last Communion of St Jerome by Sandro Botticelli', *Bulletin of The Metropolitan Museum of Art*, X (1915), pp.52-56, 72-75, 101-105.

NOTES

1 This extract is taken from the first English translation of Vasari's *Lives*, which was by Mrs. J. Foster and published by Bohn's Standard Library, 1855-64

2 This sentence reads in Italian: 'E così un quadro di Marte e Venere con i suoi amori e Vulcano, fatto con una grande arte e con una pazienza incredibile'. Mrs. Foster stresses 'E così un quadro' in her translation and refers to a single work. Panofsky rightly suggests that this ambiguous sentence refers to two separate paintings: a painting of Mars and Venus with Cupids and a painting of Vulcan.